I thoroughly recommend Sharon Dickens' new book about how we as Christians are to get on with other people. It talks about how we relate as families, neighbours and close friends and even delves into dating and marriage. It is honest about the struggles and the challenges and gives clear applications of Bible texts and gospel principles. It is packed with illustrations and an example character, Biddy, who pops up in each chapter. The language is straightforward and easy to understand for people who have recently come to faith, especially if they don't have a church background and vocabulary. At the heart of the book is Jesus, the most important relationship of all.

Graham Nicholls
Director of Affinity

So excited to see a series of books written for the purpose of discipling unchurched new believers! Dickens writes in an easy-to-read, conversational style that presents biblical truth in a highly applicable manner. Developing a biblical worldview concerning our relationships is a must for all of us, especially those who are new to the faith.

John C. Kwasny
Director of Discipleship Ministries, Pear Orchard Presbyterian
Church (PCA), Ridgeland, Mississippi
Director, One Story Ministries
Author, *Pursuing a Heart of Wisdom: Counseling Teenagers Biblically*

Relationships can be difficult and unbearable. Even as Christians, relationships aren't always pretty. Nevertheless, God wants to meet you in the brokenness of your relationships. In this book, Sharon helps us to see relationships from God's perspective, teaches us to address our own shortcomings, and points us to the power of God, alongside His people, as we navigate the brokenness of this world and the hope that is in Christ. Sharon's writing is practical, helpful, and useful in your walk with Jesus.

Kris Brossett

Pastor, Los Angeles, California

Author of *Kingdom Citizenship: Understanding God, His Plan, and Our Place in it*

RELATIONSHIPS

HOW DO I MAKE THINGS RIGHT?

SHARON DICKENS
SERIES EDITED BY MEZ MCCONNELL

IX **9Marks**

CHRISTIAN
FOCUS

Copyright © Sharon Dickens 2020
paperback ISBN 978-1-5271-0471-6
epub ISBN 978-1-5271-0543-0
mobi ISBN 978-1-5271-0544-7

10 9 8 7 6 5 4 3 2 1

Published in 2020
by
Christian Focus Publications Ltd,
Geanies House, Fearn, Ross-shire,
IV20 1TW, Great Britain.
www.christianfocus.com
Cover and interior design by Rubner Durais

Printed in China

CONTENTS

CONTENTS

PREFACE

When I first became a Christian, I didn't know anything. It was all new to me. Suddenly, this new relationship with God was supposed to change everything, especially my relationships—and to be honest, I'm not sure I was ready for it.

In hindsight, knowing what I do now, there's much I would have done differently way back when. As a young Christian I was a plank who, without real thought, shared this newfound faith I had *a bit too* enthusiastically. I loved my friends and family, and I was desperate for them to know the truth about Jesus. I was, and still am, desperate they won't go to hell. But as I said, I was a plank and I didn't share this truth well. I caused damage, hurt those I loved and left them in pain. True, I said what they needed to hear, but I lacked spiritual gentleness. My bull-in-a-china-shop approach of blurting out hard truths isn't best just because what I said was true.

Thankfully, as my relationship with God has grown deeper, He has changed me. I'm not the same person I was thirty years ago. This relationship has been the foundation that has slowly helped all the other relationships in my life change. It has taken time. But because of God, I want to be a better mum, daughter, sister, auntie and friend. He helps me see and accept the reality of my own selfish heart and plants within me a desire to love others.

I still don't have this relationship thing licked. They bring the worst and best times, sometimes all at once.

In this book, I want to help you to start to think about the relationships you have in your life. Your relationship with God will have a massive impact not only on you but also on your key relationships. Fundamentally, this new relationship with God is a game-changer.

Sharon Dickens
September 2019

SERIES INTRODUCTION

The First Steps series will help equip those from an unchurched background take the first steps in following Jesus. We call this the 'pathway to service' as we believe that every Christian should be equipped to be of service to Christ and His church no matter your background or life experience.

If you are a church leader doing ministry in hard places, use these books as a tool to help grow those who are unfamiliar with the teachings of Jesus into new disciples. These books will equip them to grow in character, knowledge and action.

Or if you yourself are new to the Christian faith, still struggling to make sense of what a Christian is, or what the Bible actually says, then this is an easy-to-understand guide as you take your first steps as a follower of Jesus.

There are many ways to use these books.

+ They could be used by an individual who simply reads through the content and works through the questions on their own.

+ They could be used in a one-to-one setting, where two people read through the material before they meet and then discuss the questions together.

+ They could be used in a group setting where a leader presents the material as a talk, stopping for group discussion throughout.

Your setting will determine how you best use this resource.

A USER'S KEY:

As you work through the studies you will come across the following symbols ...

BIDDY – I'm going to introduce you to Biddy. There will be times in each chapter when you'll hear something about her story and what's been going on in her life. We want you to take what we've been learning from the Bible and think about what difference it would make in Biddy's life and our own. So, whenever you see this symbol you'll hear a bit more about what's going on with her.

ILLUSTRATION – Through real-life examples and fake scenarios, these sections help us to understand the point that's being made.

STOP – When we hit an important or hard point we'll ask you to stop and spend some time thinking or chatting through what we've just learnt. This might be answering some questions, or it might be hearing more of Biddy's story.

KEY VERSE – The Bible is God's Word to us, and therefore it is the final word to us on everything we are to believe and how we are to behave. Therefore we want to read the Bible first, and we want to read it carefully. So whenever you see this symbol you are to read or listen to the Bible passage three times. If the person you're reading the Bible with feels comfortable, get them to read it at least once.

MEMORY VERSE – At the end of each chapter we'll suggest a Bible verse for memorisation. We have found Bible memorisation to be really effective in our context. The verse (or verses) will be directly related to what we've covered in the chapter.

SUMMARY – Also, at the end of each chapter we've included a short summary of the content of that chapter. If you're working your way through the book with another person, this might be useful to revisit when picking up from a previous week.

MEET BIDDY

One day, as you are sitting in the café, you are introduced to Biddy by her son Sean. Biddy has become a regular at the café and church. She has even been doing the Bible study 'God—Is He Out There?'[1] for weeks. If she were honest, she'd admit that she started coming mostly because she was lonely. Years ago, she lost her husband to cancer. If you asked her, she would say—even after all this time—that she's never really gotten over him dying so suddenly and leaving her on her own with the boys.

Biddy has three boys. Her oldest, Paul, is a hard worker, always watching out for her and taking her to the shops every Saturday. Paul's girlfriend, Chantelle, gets on fine with Biddy, but she isn't the biggest fan of Sean (Biddy's youngest son). She's pretty sure Sean's been stealing stuff from their flat when he's over, so now she won't have him in the house. This has caused a bit of tension between the brothers and Biddy. Paul feels like he's stuck in the middle between Sean and Chantelle. He's sick of arguing with his ma about Sean, so they just don't talk about it anymore. Willie, Biddy's middle son, never talks about it either. To be honest, he and Sean basically don't talk unless they have to, and that always bothers Biddy. She's tried to get the two of them to talk, but Willie's point-blank refused.

All she knows is something happened one night at Nanna Irene's. She'd never really seen Willie that angry before, and when she saw Sean's battered face, all bruised and smeared in blood, she was

---

1   Mez McConnell, *God—Is He Out There?* (Fearn, Scotland: Christian Focus, 2016).

totally stunned. '*Whatever it was, it had to have been bad, cause Willie's never done anything like that before. He's never caused any bother. He's the quiet one. I've even asked Sean, but it's pointless. They both refuse to talk about it.*' Biddy blames herself for all the family hassle—if only their dad was alive, he'd have knocked some sense into the three of them!

The older ones knew their dad a little, but Sean never really knew him at all. She knew that was why he had such a hard time as a kid. She broke her heart over that boy; so much potential, and now… '*I love him, but I just can't take anymore… he owes hundreds of pounds in drug debt. They are going to beat him if I can't find it.*' Last time she went to her sister for a loan. '*I just don't want to ask Dot again—she went mental last time, telling me I should kick him out. But I just can't do it, he's my son. I don't know what I'm going to do….*'

WHAT'S THE POINT?

All our relationships are in some way broken, because we all sin.

1. ARE ALL RELATIONSHIPS BROKEN IN SOME WAY?

When I say the word *relationship*, a different image will come to mind for all of us. Some will think about their husband, their wife, their mum or wee aunty Jeanie; for others it could stir up memories of their dad (that day he took them to the beach); some may instantly think of their boyfriend or girlfriend. The list is endless. In some way, shape, or form, we are all in a relationship with someone. It ranges from the most temporary of relationships—like our child's teacher—to the in-depth best friend that knows what we are thinking before we've said it. Each of these relationships will obviously be different. It's not like we're going to have the same relationship with our girlfriend as the wee man at the local shop, is it? And if we do, then there is something seriously twisted going on!

STOP

Who are you in a relationship with?

How we handle our relationships is important.

Where do we even begin with them all?

How do I handle my relationship with my son?

What kind of sister should I be?

How am I supposed to deal with the whole boyfriend thing now that I am a Christian?

More importantly, does the Bible actually have anything relevant to say?

That last question is why we are reading this book. In it, we are going to start thinking about what the Bible has to say about relationships and how we are to handle them as Christians.

Let's be frank and get the truth out there from the start: <u>all our relationships are broken</u>! 'That's mighty harsh', you might be saying. But it's a truth we can't deny. They might be good relationships, but they aren't, by any stretch of the imagination, perfect.

STOP

Just think about it for a second as you reflect on your own relationships. Pick one. What are its strengths and weaknesses?

We might be the best parent and most loving spouse anyone could ever want, but we're not perfect, and neither are our relationships. You sin. They sin. We all sin.

So, where did it all go wrong, and what's it supposed to look like?

In the beginning, God set out four basic relationships for every person.

Our relationship with Him.

How we relate to ourselves.

How we relate to other people.

How we relate to creation—the world about us.

Each of those relationships has a purpose.

> ### STOP
>
> *What do you think the purpose of each relationship is?*

+ God?

+ Myself?

+ Other people?

+ The world around me?

In our relationship with **God**, we are supposed to glorify Him. We talked about this a lot in Book 6—*Character*.[1] We are to represent God, and when people look at our lives, they should recognise who God is in us.

Simple, right? We've got that sussed! No? Me neither. At least, not all the time.

We aren't helpful to **ourselves.** We sin, and I'm not just talking about smashing through the tub of ice cream in front of the TV. We have this desire to run towards things that are bad for us and run away from what is good. We are our own biggest influencers, and we often aren't a good influence.

 'Be completely humble and gentle; be patient, bearing with one another in love. Make every effort to keep the unity of the Spirit through the bond of peace' (Eph. 4:2-3).

In **Ephesians 4:2-3,** Paul describes what our relationships with **other people** should look like. We are to be humble, gentle, patient and, to top it off, we are to put up with each other in love. Now, we might be able to pull that off *some* of the time, but not always, and certainly not with everyone. We might not want to

---

1   Sharon Dickens, *Character—How Do I Change?* (Fearn, Scotland: Christian Focus, 2019).

think about the next relationship because we know where this one is heading.

In our relationship with **the world around us**, we are supposed to take care of creation and use the resources it gives us well. No fly-tipping or litter dropping; always recycling; only shopping organically; and never buying things tested on animals. We are to eat meat from approved farms; think of our carbon footprint; never waste; weave our own cloth and sew our own clothes (made from natural fibres that are sustainable, of course). Okay, I'm being facetious, but you get my point. We are to be good caretakers of God's creation.

> **STOP**
>
> *So, what went wrong? Why do you think we are so bad at these four relationships?*

We can delude ourselves into thinking we're smashing this relationship stuff, but the trouble is, many of our relationships these days are from the safe distance of a Facebook page, Snapchat, or a text message. We find these types of relationships easier to manage. But when we think about the relationships closer to home, people we have to live and work with, we know it doesn't take long before sin rears its ugly head and has an impact. Minor offences suddenly become major infractions, and we are full of rage. Simple misunderstandings cloud the once mutual appreciation we had for one another. And, if we are not careful, our best pal walks past us in the street and acts like they don't even know us.

When Adam and Eve disobeyed God in the Garden of Eden, sin entered the world—and this has had a lasting impact upon us. It has shattered these four foundational relationships.

'But your iniquities have separated you from your God; your sins have hidden his face from you, so that he will not hear' (Isa. 59:2).

We are a flawed, sinful and broken people who, for the most part, are self-deceived and blind to our own sinfulness. We kid ourselves into thinking that we are doing alright. We tell ourselves that our relationships are not that bad. But, it's not true.

So often, being in relationships brings out the worst in us. The sad reality is that the closer the relationship, the worse we tend to be. That's when we get a glimpse of the real us. And most of the time, it's not pretty.

I realise relationships aren't all tears and tantrums. In fact, they can be amazing, fun and loving. But every relationship faces difficulties, and I know there have been times when we've all thought, *'I've had enough—I don't need this hassle anymore!'* Yet, despite this, God uses our relationships. He's using them to help us change and grow.

 ILLUSTRATION

When a blacksmith wants to shape a bit of metal, he heats it in the furnace, bashes it with a hammer, heats it some more, and then, when it's red-hot and pliable, he moulds it into the shape he wants. Without the extreme heat, metal can't be shaped. God uses our relationships like the blacksmith uses the fire. There isn't one of us who relates to everyone perfectly. Our relationships are shaped in the forge of our daily struggles.

 'What causes quarrels and what causes fights among you? Is it not this, that your passions are at war within you? You desire and do not have, so you murder. You covet and cannot obtain, so you fight and quarrel. You do not have, because you do not ask. You ask and do not receive, because you ask wrongly, to spend it on your passions' (James 4:1-3, ESV).

James doesn't mess around in this text. He gets straight to the point when he says that fights and quarrels are caused by **our desires, our lusts.** We want something we aren't getting: respect, justice, being heard, power, attention, whatever. And if we don't get what we want, we kick off in some way.

> **STOP**
>
> *What's the thing that always gets you angry? What is it you want that you're not getting?*

R .T. Kendall wrote a book called *The Way of Wisdom*. He says that what we see in James 4 *'were Christians who hadn't really come to grips with themselves, their grudges, their jealousy, their own hearts, their own lusts. They were blaming their problems on outward conditions or each other.'*[2] In other words, they were never looking at themselves. He goes on to say that in our congregations, and in our own hearts, quarrels can be traced back to our failure to set our affections on the things above: namely, Christ. Basically, he is saying that all too often our eyes are looking in the wrong direction. We too often look at ourselves and not at the Lord. R.T. Kendall goes on to reflect that it is possible to be **'outwardly moral** and **inwardly rebellious'**[3]; rotten. All goody-two-shoes on the outside, but rotten to the core inside. Kendall says that Satan doesn't care how moral we are if he can keep us torn up inside.

'Okay,' I hear you saying, *'I know I'm not perfect, but I'm not as bad as* them—*have you seen how* they *behave?'* We like to think we aren't as bad as others. We don't want to look at or admit our own rottenness. Instead, we distract ourselves by focusing on someone else. After all, there's always someone whose behaviour is worse than ours.

---

2   R. T. Kendall, *The Way of Wisdom: Patience in Waiting on God; Sermons on James 4–5* (The New Westminster Pulpit Series; Carlisle: Paternoster, 2005), p. 6.

3   Kendall, *The Way of Wisdom*, p. 3

BIDDY

Biddy was sitting at the kitchen table with Sean. They were having their dinner. *'Willie's coming over later, Sean. It'd be nice if you stayed and at least said hiya to him.'* Sean looked up at her. *'There is no way I'm staying in if he's coming over. He's two-faced and needs a good kicking! He can't keep his nose out my business. He thinks he's better than me now he's at college. Thinking he's special. He forgets I know who he is. I know the stuff he's done. He's not the wee angel you like to think, Ma. I'm having nothing to do with him.'* Biddy was stunned. She had heard Sean rant about Willie plenty of times, but this was something else.

The thing with Sean is that he doesn't realise that he's part of the problem. He's sitting at the table with his mum thinking to himself, *'Maybe I'm bad, but I'm not as bad as Willie.'* It's like the people that say, *'I may be bad, but at least I'm not as bad as a paedophile, a rapist, or a woman that beats her kids.'* Like Sean, instead of looking at our own hearts, we point the finger at somebody else.

> **STOP**
>
> *Honestly, how often do you avoid reflecting on yourself and your own sin by thinking someone else is way worse than you?*

But what about the times when someone really hurts us? Surely, they are 100% in the wrong? I know it's hard to hear, but we need to watch out that we aren't sucked into sinful destructiveness as well. Someone may behave really badly toward us, but that doesn't give us the right to be horrible back. We have to watch out that when we are sinned against, we don't respond sinfully ourselves. As Paul writes in Ephesians 4:26, 'In your anger do not sin.'

This is a difficult truth for many of us to accept because we have suffered greatly at the hands of abusers, adulterers, liars, and rumour-mongers. Of course, these things are horrendous injustices, and I'm not diminishing their seriousness. The Lord doesn't diminish them either. Every abuser will answer before the Lord for what they have done. But—and this is where it gets hard—*we cannot allow ourselves to use what has happened to us, or is happening to us, as an excuse for our own sinful behaviour.*

STOP

Do you think people are getting off lightly if you don't sort them out for the wrongs they have done to you?

 BIDDY

Sitting in front of the TV, chilling with a cup of tea, you hear the doorbell ring. When it opens you find Biddy standing on your door-step. Clearly, she's been crying. You invite her in, put the kettle on, and she starts to tell you the story. *'Sean stole from me! I can't believe he would do that—from his own mum.'*

She's also had another argument with Willie about Sean. Halfway through their fight, Willie told her why he was so angry with his brother. He'd been taking his Nanna's shopping in the back door and caught Sean stealing her engagement ring and her pension. Sean had tried to deny it, but Willie caught him. So Willie gave him a good beating. Sean begged him not to tell me and swore he wouldn't do it again.

It was the week before their Nanna died, and Willie swears Sean brought on the heart attack. *'I actually still can't believe he would do that—he loved his Nanna. Even Paul knew. Everyone knew, but me. All this time I thought the fight was over some girl they both liked. Sean swears blind he never did it. He says that Willie is lying. Now Willie is angry with me 'cause I won't kick Sean out. Even after everything I just can't kick him out. I love him. I can't make him homeless. So, Willie's stormed off and says he's done protecting me. I know this isn't Sean. It's the drugs. He loved his Nanna. I just don't know what to do. I'm trying to trust Jesus, but it doesn't make it any easier. This wouldn't have been happening if my Charlie was here. I just want it all to go away and get back to normal. I can't handle all this fighting.'*

Most of us will be thinking that Willie's right. Sean is a thieving rat and needs sorting out. True enough, the boy needs a swift kick (and Jesus). Even after Willie's initial explosive anger, he has been quietly simmering under the surface, hating his brother, having a go at him every chance he gets. His agenda when it comes to Sean is to cut him out of his life. Biddy has spent so much of her life excusing her boys' behaviour, that they've never taken responsibility for anything. She can't face the truth; she can't face making a hard decision. She just wants an easy life—for everything to go back to normal, whatever that is.

Unfortunately, Biddy is finding out the hard way that becoming a Christian doesn't mean that our problems disappear. In fact, she's going to have to learn that God uses these difficult situations to change us.

'For this very reason, make every effort to supplement your faith with virtue, and virtue with knowledge, and knowledge with self-control, and self-control with steadfastness, and steadfastness with godliness, and godliness with brotherly affection, and brotherly affection with love. For if these qualities are yours and are increasing, they keep you from being ineffective or unfruitful in the knowledge of our Lord Jesus Christ' (2 Pet. 1:5-8, ESV).

Make every effort, it says in verse 5. Let's not be fooled. Relationships require hard work

    —even when we're Christians,

    perhaps *especially* when we're Christians.

It's not like God waves some magic fairy dust over us and we all become amazing people overnight. As Christians, the control sin once had over us has been broken by Jesus. Through faith in Him, we have been set free. But—and this is a big but—**our old sinful nature, we sometimes call it the 'old self', remains and puts up a real fight.** We see this fight play out in how we handle our relationships.

The old self wants to use our words as a vicious weapon instead of speaking words of encouragement, peace, or even keeping quiet. The old self wants to hold on to bitterness and grudges instead of forgiving wrongs. When we reject the opportunity either to forgive or ask for forgiveness, our relationships suffer. Relationships are hard. And yet, God requires us to be **imitators of Jesus** in the midst of the struggles. Now that's a smack in the teeth! Our relationships aren't about us, but about how we imitate Jesus in them.

To be able to do that effectively, Biddy is going to need help to fix her eyes on Christ, rely on Him, and resist the temptation to excuse or hide from her sin. She might not have the strength to do this on her own—but thankfully, she doesn't have to. For the Christian, we can look to Jesus for help to change from the inside out, rely on Him, and resist the temptation to give in to the old self.

As a new Christian, it can be difficult to imitate Christ when we are still trying to work out who He is. Let's face it, we're new to this Christian lark and not quite sure how it all works. That's why it's helpful to find godly, mature Christians from church to model Jesus to us. Thankfully, Biddy has Mona to help her navigate what the Bible has to say about what's going on in her life.

KEY POINT

All our relationships are, in some way, broken. You sin. They sin. We all sin. But, as Christians, God wants to use these relationships to change us and to help us model Jesus.

MEMORY VERSE

'God is our refuge and strength, an ever-present help in trouble. Therefore we will not fear' (Ps. 46:1-2a).

SUMMARY

We excuse, justify, and pretend we aren't as bad as the next guy. We think we are great at relationships, but secretly we have our own agendas kicking off in the background. All too often, we just want an easy life and our own way. If we took an honest look inside ourselves, we aren't even a shadow of the image of Jesus, never mind being imitators of Him.

WHAT'S THE POINT?

Being a Christian is hard and we need help understanding our new life.

2. ACCOUNTABILITY (ONE TO ONE)

It's helpful to have a mature Christian who knows the Bible well there to help us. Relationships like these are vital. They can be called many things: a discipling relationship, a mentor, a one-to-one or accountability partner. Whatever we call them, these relationships help us recognise when our own agendas are kicking off in the background, as we thought about in chapter one. They help us take an honest look at ourselves so that we recognise how we can be imitators of Christ. They will help us navigate the Bible, work out who Jesus is, and help us apply His Word to our lives. This person needs to be a godly, mature, and seasoned Christian. We need more than just our pal who's been a Christian for five minutes—that would be the blind leading the blind.

> **STOP**
>
> *How do you think you would manage navigating the Christian faith without anyone helping you?*

 BIDDY

Biddy and Mona are sitting in the café. Biddy says *'I banged into May the other day. She was off to do her one-to-one with Lynn. She asked me who's my one-to-one. I didn't know what she was talking about, and when she started telling me it just sounded weird, people asking you questions they have no right to. Just blooming nosey if you ask me.'* It was at this point Mona started laughing, and then said

'Remember when the kids were small? Did you ever teach them how to bake fairy cakes? It was one of my favourite things with the kids, baking fairy cakes and watching them fight over who got to lick the bowl.'

Biddy smiles before she responds: *'Aye, those were the days when they actually still liked each other. Ha ha… Willie always liked the icing. I'm sure that, most of the time, more went in his mouth than on the cakes.'*

Pausing for a few seconds, the two ladies chuckled as they sipped their tea. Mona continued, *'But, I bet you showed them how to make those cakes. You didn't just expect them to work it out for themselves. You probably got the recipe book out, showed them how to measure everything, beat the batter, and fold in the flour. Can you imagine what the cakes would have looked like if you didn't guide them through it and teach them how? Having a one-to-one is a bit like that. It's just an older, mature Christian teaching a younger Christian what the Bible has to say about life. They help them walk through it—it's like having someone to ask the hard questions of, while they also point you in the right direction.'*

> **STOP**
>
> *Do you have a relationship like this? If so, how helpful has that relationship been to you, especially in the early days of being a Christian? If you don't, why not?*

To be honest, the Bible doesn't actually have a verse I can point to that specifically says you need to have a one-to-one relationship. But, there are some principles that basically say it's a good thing for older, mature Christians to teach and show the younger ones how to be grown up, mature Christians. To teach them to follow

Christ just like we mentioned in First Steps Book 6[1] when we talked about having a solid Christian character.

'Likewise, teach the older women to be reverent in the way they live, not to be slanderers or addicted to much wine, but to teach what is good. Then they can urge the younger women to love their husbands and children, to be self-controlled and pure, to be busy at home, to be kind, and to be subject to their husbands, so that no one will malign the word of God' (Titus 2:3-5).

> **STOP**
>
> *What does Titus specifically tell the older, mature Christian to do for the younger ones? And what seems to be the point of the whole exercise?*

We can have some proper wacky ideas about what a Christian looks like—how we think they are supposed to

behave,

dress,

and talk.

Some of the ideas we have in our heads are just outright wrong and need rethinking.

When I was a young Christian, I was told a bunch of unhelpful guff about the Bible, Jesus, demons, and the Holy Spirit. To be honest, it messed with my head a bit. At first, I thought that everything people told me was true just because they had been a Christian longer than me. Thankfully, an older, mature Christian helped me sort through the guff and pointed me to what the Bible actually said. She patiently helped me unpack all the myths and legends, teaching me what was true. She was a good sounding-board.

---

1   Dickens, *Character—How Do I Change?*

STOP

What guff have you been told that you're not quite sure is true?

When we are young Christians, we can mistakenly think that everyone who is older in the faith must know everything. This might shock you, but not everyone who has been a Christian for years is mature and wise.

> They might look the part on the surface, but if you look closely, you can see clearly that they aren't a great example or ambassador for Jesus.

> They may be able to spout a ton of biblical-sounding words, but you start to notice they don't take it to heart—they don't seem to apply the Bible to their lives.

> They might be old, maybe they've even been Christians for twenty years, but they haven't grown in their faith much and aren't remotely mature.

You want to give this type of Christian a wide berth when it comes to your one-to-one. If they aren't growing in their own faith, how can they help you grow in yours?

 ### BIDDY

Biddy had started going to the Bible study on Wednesday night. She felt a bit overwhelmed at first; they all seemed to know so much more than her. She found Mez explained the Bible in a way even she could understand but, even though she had questions, she still wasn't brave enough to say them out loud. The last couple of weeks, Biddy walked home with Flora and they talked about what they had learnt that night. Biddy had watched Flora do that holy sway thing Christians did when the songs started on Sunday morning. She even prayed big, massive prayers with some fancy Bible words. She clearly knew loads. Sometimes, though, Flora just confused Biddy. She seemed to be really confident and knew a lot, but it was like sometimes she said something a bit different than what they'd heard at the study. Biddy figured she was just being a bit stupid.

This night had been hard; Mez was talking about forgiveness and the unity of believers. Flora had asked lots of questions, and at one point had been debating with Mez about something he said until he shut her down and moved on. She wasn't pleased at all; you could see it written all over her face. She was raging, and wouldn't shut up about it on the way home. *'I don't agree with everything that he said tonight. How can you forgive someone if they haven't even asked for forgiveness or admitted they've sinned against you? They need to repent first so you can forgive them. I'm not convinced being spiritually united means we have to spend time with them, because God is very clear about "Bad company corrupting good character." We need to be wise about who we are spending our time with. I mean we aren't even supposed to "eat with the slanderer," never mind unite with them. The only relationship we need to pay attention to is our personal one with Jesus—we are united to Him alone. Everything else is just a worldly distraction, and we need to make sure we protect ourselves from unhelpful influence.'*

On the surface, Flora looks like a grown-up Christian. But even though she uses lots of spiritual phrases, it was only on the surface. She talked a good game, but it was all hot air. Sometimes those that speak the most and the loudest aren't the ones we should be listening to.

STOP

Who would you spend time with one-to-one: Biddy, Flora, or Mona? Why?

STOP

What do you think a mature Christian looks like? What should you be looking for? List your top five things:

1.

2.

3.

4.

5.

Some people know the Bible, but aren't actually that hot about applying God's Word to their lives. These people are all knowledge and no application.

It's like they've met Jesus, but don't actually get to know Him.

 'Anyone who listens to the word but does not do what it says is like someone who looks at his face in a mirror and, after looking at himself, goes away and immediately forgets what he looks like' (James 1:23-24).

Don't get me wrong, I'm not saying that mature Christians are perfect and know everything. But you want to see:

someone who is quick to ask for forgiveness,

someone who is growing,

someone who wants to make God the centre of their lives.

 BIDDY

It seems natural that Mona should meet with Biddy because they've been friends from the off. It was Mona's own accountability partner—Miriam—who had to persuade her to consider discipling Biddy. *'What if she asks me a really hard question I can't answer?'* Mona asked Miriam. *'Do you not think she'd be better with*

you? You know a lot more about the Bible than I do. She'd prefer you.' Miriam encouraged Mona to step up and speak to Biddy. Thankfully, Mona agreed and spoke to Biddy the next time they were together.

'Biddy, do you remember the other week when you banged into May and we were talking about having a one-to-one relationship? Well, I wondered if you fancied doing one-to-one with me? I mean, I see you most days but, it would mean that we'd study the Bible together and ask the accountability questions[2]—what do you think?'

Biddy was quiet for a long time, in fact, it got a bit awkward there for a moment, but then she said, *'What kind of questions? I heard Sarah talking last week about Claire asking them and how horrific it was to get busted. I don't think I'm up for that to be honest.'* Mona nearly gave up, thinking Miriam would definitely be better at answering this than her, but eventually she thought she'd better give it a go. *'Well, the elders have this list of questions and, you're right, some of them are difficult. It's not that they are hard just because, but they are there to help us reflect on how we are doing spiritually, and also to think through how we are responding to people. They make you think is all. Sometimes, that's about hard things you might not want to face, but should. Like, one of the questions is, "Is there anyone you need to forgive or ask forgiveness from?" 80% of the time, it's not a hard question. But those times you're raging inside at Sean or you've spoken harshly to Willie, it gets uncomfortable because you're challenged by the answer. Does that make sense?'*

STOP

Is there anyone you need to forgive or ask forgiveness from?

---

2   20schemesWomen accountability questions are available by emailing <women@20schemes.com>.

Mona continued, 'In one-to-one, we study the Bible and then think about how we apply what we've been learning to our lives. Then we discuss the questions.' Biddy looked at her and asked, 'What other questions are there?'

Let's reflect on a few of the accountability questions Mona will ask Biddy. How would you answer them?

> Is there any sin you love too much to repent of?
>
> Has your use of social media—time spent on it and what you've posted—honoured Jesus?
>
> What has been more important to you than God in the last week?

I have had an accountability partner for over a decade and it seems normal, natural, and essential to me now. But to be honest, I didn't feel like that at first. There was a bit of me that was thinking: 'No way am I sharing my deepest, darkest secrets with anyone!' It just felt weird. Then I had a word with myself.

If I truly wanted to grow, if I wanted my heart to be challenged, then I had to step up and make a conscious effort.

I want to be honest with you; it took time to establish the relationship. Even with a desire to be honest, a will to change, and a desire to set a good example for those around me, it took about two years before we had an unguarded, honest, and vulnerable conversation.

Trust takes time to build, but it's worth the effort.

So, at first, it may feel fake and contrived. It will take time for you to feel comfortable opening up, especially to someone you don't know that well. We're not saying that having a one-to-one is like having someone be your 'priest' or 'confessor', but they are a helpful resource, a guide, and a spiritual friend who points you in the right direction.

STOP

Ask yourself, are you serious about growing as a Christian? Are you?

 'The heart is deceitful above all things and beyond cure. Who can understand it?' (Jer. 17:9).

I know this is hard. Often, we aren't even honest with ourselves! As Jeremiah says here, we don't understand most of the time what's really going on in our own hearts. But it's really the only way we will see lasting and real change.

Pray and ask God for wisdom when looking for an accountability partner.

Ask your elders or women's worker for suggestions in order to help you make a wise choice.

 BIDDY

Mona looks at Biddy and says, *'So, give me it straight: What's really putting you off one-to-one?'* Biddy laughs, *'I swear you've got mind-reading abilities. I'm just wondering how confidential this is. Like, if I tell you something, do you have to tell the elders what I've been saying?'*

STOP

What do you think confidentiality looks like? Are there any times where you think it's right for confidentiality to be broken?

Before you start to do one-to-one, make sure you lay the ground rules.

Think about confidentiality and what the policy is for your church (they will have one).

Think through the questions you want to be asked, especially ones that address hard issues.

STOP

What is the one question you would hate to be asked?

STOP

Why don't you want to be asked this?

We all have something we want to hide from—things in our past, or some sin we're ashamed about. In time, God will challenge you, convict you. You'll know He wants you to deal with it.

We don't have to face these moments on our own.

KEY POINT

We all need a mature Christian who will invest in our lives to point us to Jesus, pray with us, and help us accept responsibility for applying God's Word to our lives every day.

 MEMORY VERSE

'Therefore confess your sins to each other and pray for each other so that you may be healed. The prayer of a righteous person is powerful and effective' (James 5:16).

 SUMMARY

Remember, just because a person has been going to church for fifty years doesn't make them a mature Christian. It just makes them old! We don't want someone who isn't fully committed to their local church either. We want someone who is in the relationship for the long haul—someone who has accepted the responsibility of church membership and is under the authority of the elders and fellow members. When we become Christians, our most important relationship is with the Lord. But it's helpful for all Christians to have other godly, mature Christians point us to Christ so that He remains front and centre of our lives.

WHAT'S THE POINT?

Jesus should be the most important relationship in our lives.

3. CHRIST FRONT AND CENTRE

STOP

What are your five most important relationships?

I hope that God is mentioned in your list. But has He made it to the top of the list?

Does God come before our family?

Our relationship with God has to be number one in our lives. I realise, for a lot of people, hearing this will be a real struggle. I've heard people say things like, *'I love God, but my kids come first!'*

We can so easily think that if we put God first that means, in some way, our relationship with our family isn't as important.

We feel as though we are admitting we love them less. Our thinking can get twisted on this. Yet, if we make God our number one priority, this actually helps us to love our family and others far more *than we ever thought possible.*

We become a better mum, dad, kid, and sister. How is that even possible?

This is what we are going to look at in this chapter: why God needs to be our number one relationship, and how we can make that happen.

STOP

If we really lived as if God were our number one, what would that look like?

If God truly were number one in our lives, then it would be clear by our behaviour. For instance, the minute we got up in the morning we'd be desperate to see what He had to say in His Word.

We'd read the Bible with passion.

We'd want to pray all the time.

We'd trust Him and never doubt.

We'd obey every command without a word of objection.

When our pals and family look at us, they'd see a changed person.

Instead, I suspect that the reality is somewhat different. When we wake up, all too often we are desperate to see what everyone has said on Facebook.

We check our comments on Twitter.

We scroll through our likes on Instagram.

We check our emails.

We respond to the texts, WhatsApps, or Snapchats we've had through the night.

The sad reality is that it's probably going to take the first meltdown of the day to make us think about God and our need to talk to Him.

There are times in life when we are just happy to survive the day in one piece without one of the kids getting hurt or us snapping at someone.

Truthfully, we fall short.

There always seems to be something getting in the way of spending time with God. Whether it's taking the kids somewhere, meeting up with friends, shopping, cooking, cleaning, working, running errands—the list is endless. To put it bluntly, we say we want to make God a priority in life, but what actually happens is very different. This is the heart of the problem.

STOP

In the busyness and chaos of life, how can we protect our relationship with God?

 'Above all else, guard your heart, for everything you do flows from it' (Prov. 4:23).

 ILLUSTRATION

Recently, I went to visit my brother in South Africa during a water drought. We were allowed a three-minute shower per day, and we had to conserve all the water we could. In fact, my brother went as far as building a wooden box with a plastic liner to stand in whilst showering. This was to collect shower water for re-use in the garden. Disgusting, I know, yet very effective.

For me in the UK, it's hard to imagine how precious water is when it falls out of the sky so regularly! But even in the UK, we hear of water shortages and hose-pipe bans. Unlike parts of Africa that are desperate for water to live, the main worry we have isn't whether or not the water comes out of the tap, but how pure and filtered it is. Even for the short time I was in South Africa, I knew from the news and radio that if they didn't get rain soon they'd run out of water within weeks. It was like a massive doomsday countdown. If that were the UK, we would be stockpiling water and there'd be riots in supermarkets. And you can be sure that when the tap did run dry, those with a hidden stockpile would guard it like life depended on it—because it would!

We find exactly this same feeling in **Proverbs 4:23**. It teaches that we are to guard our hearts, for everything we do flows from it. In fact, our very lives depend on it.

 'Then he taught me, and he said to me, "Take hold of my words with all your heart; keep my commands, and you will live"' (Prov. 4:4).

We see this again in **Proverbs 4:4**. There's no escaping the importance of our relationship with God. It's a matter of life and death. In a book I was reading recently, the author Ray Ortlund put it like this: *'Your heart has a hunger, a thirst, that only Christ can satisfy.'*[1]

The problem for many of us is that we try to satisfy our thirst with the wrong things, and nothing satisfies us for very long. *We just end up craving more and more.*

 ILLUSTRATION

Sometimes I wake up in the morning and all I fancy for my dinner is a big, fat, juicy fish supper with lashings of brown sauce. I think about it all day. I crave it. I look forward to it. I even plan what I'm going to watch on the TV whilst eating it. But many days, dinnertime comes and all I get to eat is a salad. Well, it's not the same, is it? I'll eat, and my hunger will be satisfied because I have been fed. But my craving for that fish hasn't been satisfied. In fact, I'm disappointed, and so I spend the rest of the night thinking about a fish supper I never had.

In a similar way, trying to replace our thirst for Jesus with anything else is as satisfying as drinking a glass of sand when we're gasping

---

1   Ray Ortlund, *Proverbs: Wisdom that Works* (Preaching the Word; Wheaton, IL: Crossway), p. 87.

for a drink of cold water. Or being given a salad when all we want is a fish with brown sauce!

STOP

Take a few seconds just to think back on the last time you gave in to a temptation like lust or greed. Did it satisfy?

When we give in to our temptations and lusts, they often bring immediate relief and gratification. But as we know, it's only temporary, and so we find ourselves chasing the same things again and again. We lie to ourselves, thinking, *'This time it will satisfy. This will be the last time.'*

Instead, we end up wanting more and more, and so we chase more.

When this happens, our desires have become more important to us than God.

We call this **idol worship**. John Calvin calls our hearts *'a perpetual factory of idols'* because we are constantly thirsting after something, anything, other than God.[2]

 ILLUSTRATION

When I try to think about the image of a factory, I can't get past *Willie Wonka and the Chocolate Factory.*[3] No points for guessing what's been influencing my thoughts! But it actually gives us a great practical insight into the idol factories of our hearts. Augustus Gloop's lust for chocolate leads him to fall into the chocolate river and get lodged in the pipes. Veruca Salt's desire

---

2   <https://www.ccel.org/ccel/calvin/institutes.txt> accessed 27th August 2019.

3   Roald Dahl and David Seltzer, *Willie Wonka and The Chocolate Factory* (Warner Home Video. 2005). Based on the Roald Dahl book *Charlie and the Chocolate Factory.*

for everything leads her to be rejected and sent down the 'bad egg' chute to the incinerator. In the book, we read how each character ignores all the warning signs—they do what they want anyway, only to face the consequences.

Of course, our hearts and our desires are subtler than Augustus' and Veruca's. Unlike theirs, our hearts' desires are usually unseen. But don't be fooled. They are there, carefully hidden, and they affect everything we do. No matter how hard we try, we can't hide from God; He knows what truly rules our hearts.

 1 Corinthians 4:5 says, '*He will bring to light what is hidden in darkness and will expose the motives of the heart.*'

 '*For if we go on sinning deliberately after receiving the knowledge of the truth, there no longer remains a sacrifice for sins, but a fearful expectation of judgement, and a fury of fire that will consume the adversaries*' (Heb. 10:26-27, ESV).

We need to heed these warnings early. Remember Proverbs 4:4, '*Then he taught me, and he said to me, "Take hold of my words with all your heart; keep my commands, and you will live."*' Our relationship with God matters because, without Him, we could end up throwing in the towel and walking away from our faith.

 '*But because of your hard and impenitent heart you are storing up wrath for yourself on the day of wrath when God's righteous judgement will be revealed*' (Rom. 2:5, ESV).

 BIDDY

Imagine flicking through Facebook and seeing a post about a wee old couple whose house has been robbed. You see a horrendous picture of wee Alice's face all bashed and bruised. You read the responses and plan to nip in to see them on the way home. Suddenly, a few of the comments catch your eye. Sean's name has been mentioned as a person of interest. You know Biddy is going to be devastated when she hears this news. She seems to have been really struggling lately, and even though you've tried to work out what's going on, you've had no joy. You put your coat on and head over to see wee Alice, not realising Biddy has more on her mind that you could ever know…

'…Ma, I need you to listen to me. There are some crazy rumours flying round about me. You know I wouldn't do anything like that. I swear, Ma. But the police want to stitch me up. You know they've been after me for ages. I need you to tell them I was in with you all night.'

This was the exact moment Biddy realised that what everyone had been telling her about Sean was true. He had ripped off his Nanna and poor Alice. He'd actually smashed wee Alice in the face. She was sick to her stomach. She had to lie for him. There was no choice. She couldn't turn her own flesh and blood in. But what would God think about that? She's a Christian now. Isn't she supposed to be honest? But she has to protect her boy. She's his mum, after all…

It was clear in that moment that she had a choice: God or Sean. Being a Christian just seemed too hard. God asked too much. That following Sunday was the first service Biddy had missed in months. She just couldn't face it. One Sunday became two, then three. Now she hasn't been near church, the Bible study, or God in months. When you chat to her she says, 'I still love God and that, I just do it in my own way.'

Sadly, I've known many people who have claimed to be Christians but walked away. It's not like they just got up one morning and decided to throw in the towel. Like Biddy, it happened over time, bit by bit, little by little, a wee compromise here, a lie there. Slowly, they squished down their conscience and began making choices that were more like their old self. No matter how much we tried, they simply ignored our warnings and continued on the sinful path back to their old life until, over the course of time, their heart became hardened to the truth they used to profess.

 'Give careful thought to the paths for your feet and be steadfast in all your ways. Do not turn to the right or the left; keep your foot from evil' (Prov. 4:26-27).

Proverbs 4 reminds me a lot of Psalm 1, which talks about two paths. The path of the righteous which leads to flourishing, and the path of the wicked which leads to destruction. There isn't an in-between detour or a skirting-round-the-edge bypass. We guard our heart and relationship with God by making sure we're on the right path. Proverbs is saying: *Engage your brain. Carefully think about what you are doing. Be deliberate where you step.* No matter what we want to tell ourselves, we don't stray from the path by accident. Instead, it's one step at a time away from God.

 'wisdom preserves the life of him who has it' (Eccles. 7:12b, ESV).

We receive many things from God, and one of them is His wisdom. Without God, we are fools, heading away from Him. *'The fool says in his heart, "There is no God." They are corrupt, their deeds are vile; there is no one who does good'* (Ps. 14:1). Without God, we would all be fools. The fool replaces God with other things.

Wisdom means not relying on ourselves, but on God.

 BIDDY

'I get that my relationship with God is important, but I'm not understanding why He has to be number one. My boys mean everything to me. They have already lost so much. I don't understand why God would want them to mean less to me than He does. My loyalty has to be to them first. How can I be a good mum if I put anyone before them? I think God is asking for too much, and it's just not fair.'

STOP

Are you like Biddy? You get that God is important, but should your family come first?

We need to start playing the long game. What do I mean by this? Simply that it's our relationship with God that changes us and helps us to grow. He transforms us from the inside-out as we become more like Jesus.

As a result, we become more loving, kind, honest, faithful, patient, and even gentle.

We start to display self-control instead of screaming like a banshee at the kids.

We start living with integrity instead of lying.

We are different, and it's not just for a week or two.

We actually start to become better parents, sisters, and brothers through God's work in us—and people notice.

Get it? Making God number one helps us to make everyone else *more* of a priority, not less, because we become less selfish and more selfless.

STOP

Do we spend time getting close to God?

We may have a bunch of legitimate excuses, but the harsh reality is that everyone reading this has enough time to be spending some of our allotted 1,440 minutes per day with God.

But the harsh truth is that we always make time for whatever we really want to do. It's as simple as that.

We need to plan, discipline ourselves, and make the necessary sacrifices.

+ **Plan** – We need to carve out the time. Basically, we have to get our backsides into gear.

+ **Disciplined** – Are we sticking to the plan even when life gets in the way, or are we being lazy?

+ **Desire** – If we are being honest, sometimes we just can't be bothered, or we just go through the motions.

+ **Focus** – No interruptions, no phone, no distractions.

+ **Sacrifice** – Something has to give. Whatever it takes, we need to make it happen.

+ **Making good choices** – What we watch, read, and pay attention to feeds our heart.

Proverbs 4:24-25 says, '*Keep your mouth free of perversity; keep corrupt talk far from your lips. Let your eyes look straight ahead; fix your gaze directly before you.*' Proverbs brings attention to our eyes and mouth for a reason. One feeds our heart, and the other reveals our heart.

 '*For where your treasure is, there your heart will be also*' (Matt. 6:21).

Most of all, we need to remember who we are now: **children of God.** We are in this precious new relationship with God because of what Christ has done on the cross.

 '*See what great love the Father has lavished on us, that we should be called children of God! And that is what we are! The reason the world does not know us is that it did not know him. Dear friends, now*

we are children of God, and what we will be has not yet been made known. But we know that when Christ appears, we shall be like him, for we shall see him as he is' (1 John 3:1-2)

STOP

Have you grasped the enormity of being called a child of God?

KEY POINT

Jesus needs to be the most important relationship in our lives because, when He is, we change and grow, and all our other relationships are better. He needs to be the most important relationship because it keeps us close to Him and protects us from the danger of walking away from God, which has serious eternal consequences.

 ## MEMORY VERSE

'Then he taught me, and he said to me, "Take hold of my words with all your heart; keep my commands, and you will live"' (Prov. 4:4).

 ## SUMMARY

When we make God the number one priority in our life, He helps us to love our family and others far *more than we ever thought possible.* He changes us and helps us to grow. He transforms us from the inside-out as we become more like Jesus, helping us to become a *better mum, dad, kid, sister, or brother.* Making God number one helps us to make everyone else more of a priority, not less, because we become less selfish and more selfless—more Christlike.

WHAT'S THE POINT?

God uses the community around us to change us and help us grow.

4. NO MAN'S AN ISLAND

We live in a culture that's very much about the individual. The big 'I' is number one. 'I' has become so prominent that it's almost like an idol, more important to us than God. It even affects how we view our relationship with God. So, instead of making God number one, we totally twist our relationship with Him to be all about us.

> **STOP**
>
> *How would this thinking affect our view of things like Sunday service or church membership?*

When it's all about 'me', we can think that we don't need anyone but ourselves. This isn't helpful. Besides, it's a lie.

God has made us to glorify Him, but also to be in community with others.

So there's no perfect excuse for missing church, isolating ourselves, and worrying only about ourselves. In this chapter, we're going to look at how God brings about change in us through our relationships. Relationships aren't all plain sailing, but God uses them to reveal what needs to change in us.

ILLUSTRATION

I heard this illustration from David Powlison. Imagine you are holding a plastic bottle, half-full of water. Now, if you take the lid off and shake it really hard, what's going to happen? The water's going to go all over the place, right? You're going to end up soaking wet. So, the question he asks is this: Why does the water come out of the bottle? Everyone says, 'Because you shook it.' NO. The water comes out because it was inside the bottle in the first place.

Nice story, but what's that got to do with us? Think of yourself as the plastic bottle. The water is our hidden sin that's deep inside. When we do life with people and they get on our nerves or hurt us, that's the shaking of the bottle. The hidden sin comes to the surface and spills out because it was there in the first place.

That hidden sin tears us away from God, puts us at odds with others, and makes us self-reliant.

That's only one angle. Relationships have more to offer than simply bringing our hidden sin to the surface. We have this whole love-hate thing going on with relationships. We often run away from them, but they're also worth the effort. There's much more to them, such as discipleship, friendship, encouragement, comfort, laughter, support—the list is endless.

STOP

Think about your closest relationships. How close are they? Do you go deeper than just 'I'm okay,' or do you keep people at arm's length because you're self-reliant, not wanting to ask for help?

Many of us find it difficult to share the truth about our struggles. We never seem to get beyond the fake face we portray. We paste it on and make sure everyone knows we are fine, especially when we aren't. Whether from

polite habit,

repressed emotions,

pride,

privacy,

or self-preservation,

our individualistic attitude has a massive impact on us. It's hard facing up to the deep-rooted sin in our lives.

Think back to chapter 2 on one-to-ones: honesty, openness, and sharing help us endure what's going on because we can support, encourage, and pray effectively for one another.

 'Let us hold unswervingly to the hope we profess, for he who promised is faithful. And let us consider how we may spur one another on toward love and good deeds, not giving up meeting together, as some are in the habit of doing, but encouraging one another—and all the more as you see the Day approaching' (Heb. 10:23-25).

 BIDDY

Biddy struggled to make friends in church. People are weird, at least to her. They seem to be really friendly and ask interesting questions, but it's like they don't really listen, and they never answer any of Biddy's questions. But Mona was different. Biddy liked her instantly.

In the beginning, they started meeting up for coffee and a scone every week to have a wee natter . Mona saves a seat for Biddy on a Sunday morning. She quietly answers Biddy's questions throughout the service, eventually taking on her one-to-one.

Mona was the first to notice that Biddy had missed a Sunday service. She got worried and texted her. Even though Biddy seems to be missing more and more at church, she still meets up with Mona weekly. It is at one of these coffee dates that Mona plucks up the courage to say, 'Biddy, I've been praying about this all week. I'm so worried I'll say the wrong words, but I have to say it. I'm really concerned about you missing church. You tell me all the time that you love Jesus, but you aren't doing what He wants you to. You need to be spending time at church to hear the sermon and to hang out with Christians. Why are you avoiding us? Has someone said something to you?'

Mona can have this necessary conversation because of her relationship with Biddy. Something is going on with her, and hopefully she will be open to Mona and tell her about it. Like Biddy, we hide the truth, deceive ourselves, and rarely want to admit it. We are our own worst enemies. We prefer to live in secret, and not to have to care for anyone but ourselves. But when we do that, we end up like Biddy, trying to avoid both God and the people of God.

To be fair, not everyone keeps their sin hidden. There are those who tell anyone who will listen everything that has gone on, all the gory details. If this is you, trust me, it's not helpful. There may be a time when you will even regret it. We need to be wise with what we share.

STOP

Are you being wise about what you share and who you share it with? Have you ever shared something you now wished you kept quiet about? Why?

Think of the church as a new family. Our congregations can pray, support, model maturity, strengthen one another, bring comfort, admonish, and, ultimately, point us to Christ. And as family, we are now responsible to one another.

STOP

What would you say to Biddy when she says, 'I'm a Christian and I read the Bible and that, but I don't need church. I can do this on my own'?

 'If one member suffers, all suffer together; if one member is honoured, all rejoice together.' (1 Cor. 12:26, ESV).

Have you ever had to watch a member of your family go through something terrible? You feel the hurt, anguish, and worry. You feel their pain as you suffer with them. It's the same with your new church family.

When one member suffers, we all suffer.

We can think that our decisions only affect us. But that's not what 1 Corinthians 12:26 says. All our decisions and the things that happen to us affect the whole church. At this point, I feel like I should break into the *High School Musical* song 'We're All in This Together'[1], because this is how it is now. You matter to your new church family, and they should matter to you.

 'But encourage one another daily, as long as it is called "Today", so that none of you may be hardened by sin's deceitfulness.' (Heb. 3:13).

KEY POINT

We don't like it, but God uses the people in our lives to change us. When we do life together, God uses the inevitable skirmishes to bring our hidden sin to the surface. This gives us the chance to deal with our sin, and to love and care for each other better. The

---

1   'We're All in This Together.' Theme song to the movie *High School Musical* (Walt Disney, 2006).

way we love each other as Christians says a lot about who God is to our non-Christian family and friends.

MEMORY VERSE

'*You can trust a friend who corrects you, but kisses from an enemy are nothing but lies.*' (Prov. 27:6, CEV).

SUMMARY

We like to think that we don't need anyone, but we haven't been made that way. God made us to need Him and other people. No Christian is an island, and no church has only one member. The church is our new family. No matter how much we want it to be different, we are responsible to one another as a family of believers.

WHAT'S THE POINT?

We must learn to face up to trials and struggles in a godly way.

5. WHEN IT ALL GOES WRONG

There was a TV advert for an insurance company years ago. The basic story was that something unexpected had happened, and the family's life as they knew it was about to be altered for good. As the penny dropped for them all, the dad suddenly broke into song: '*There may be trouble ahead...*' just as the caption came up with the insurance company logo and the subtitle, '*For the life you don't yet know.*'

It's true, we don't yet know what's ahead, but I'm absolutely certain of one thing: we all have to face some sort of trouble, trial, or hardship. Some will be no fault of our own; we can't do anything to prevent it. But other trials may be self-inflicted, like if we drink too much and end up with cirrhosis of the liver—or we keep on maxing out our credit card and getting deeper and deeper into debt.

'Dear friends, do not be surprised at the fiery ordeal that has come on you to test you, as though something strange were happening to you.' (1 Pet. 4:12).

'For it has been granted to you that for the sake of Christ you should not only believe in him but also suffer for his sake' (Phil. 1:29, ESV).

I know, I know, it's depressing!

So why am I telling you all this? Do I just like raining on your parade? No, of course not. Have you heard of the saying **'forewarned is forearmed'**? My mum uses it all the time. It means, to have prior knowledge of possible dangers gives you a tactical advantage. Basically, if we know something is likely to happen, then it helps us prepare, stand firm, and be ready to endure.

 ILLUSTRATION

As I'm writing this, there have been weather warnings because of snow. Currently, we have a red snow alert and are being told not to travel because of the danger. 'Don't travel,' they say, 'unless it's an emergency, and then be prepared for the journey by putting blankets, water, and food in the car.' It's been on every news station; in fact, BBC Scotland had an extended news night to cover the snow news and disruption. Even with all the bulletins, radio alerts, and Facebook posts warning people the snow was coming, the evening news has still been filled with people stranded in their cars overnight for up to fifteen hours in freezing temperatures. Many were without provisions or even enough petrol to keep their engines ticking over for heat. Emergency crews battled to rescue them. And yet, this morning, even with the warnings still in place, people are ignoring them and heading towards the motorway in their cars.

One of the ways to be prepared is to think about how we deal with struggles when they come. Unfortunately, sometimes the way we deal with things can cause us just as much hassle.

 BIDDY

'I know you did it. I can't believe you would hurt Alice. You've known her all your life! She was so good to me when your dad died. She was good to us—especially you! YOU broke in and beat her. I don't even know who you are.'

Sean just looks at her and says, '*You don't know what you're talking about. You know I was here, I couldn't have done it.*' He laughs as he walks out the door.

He is right. She's made her bed and now she has to lie in it. She couldn't have told on Sean. She just couldn't. Biddy sits at the kitchen table and cries. She feels so alone. She misses the church and Mona, but she just can't go back. '*It's all my fault. I've caused this. He wouldn't have done anything like this if his dad was alive. I just wasn't enough.*' Biddy does what she always does when it gets too much. She shuts the door and shuts out the world. She takes a couple extra pills tonight '*just to help me sleep.*'

> **STOP**
>
> *Biddy's go-to habits for dealing with stress aren't helpful for her or Sean. How about you? What is your go-to response? How do you respond when life gets stressful?*

Are you the type that pretends things are fine and always puts on a brave face, or do you escape with too much TV, X-Box, food, or drugs?

Or are you the total martyr, exaggerating everything that's going on, saying to yourself, 'No one, and I mean no one, suffers more than me'?

Are you the prickly and hypersensitive type? You know who you are—you're all defensive and self-protective. You're the sort that slam-bangs your way through your day, making sure everyone around you knows you're having a hard time.

Maybe you're the bitter and angry type, re-running a scene in your head, working out what you should've said or how to get them back with a sharp one-liner.

Maybe you're the quitter who gives up even at the smallest hurdle, or you make excuses for yourself. We all have different ways of dealing with stress, and the chances are that you recognise yourself in more than one of the examples.

Like I said, sometimes the way we deal with stress can cause us just as much hassle. Sometimes the way that we deal with stress is downright sinful.

We need to pay attention to how we respond when pressure comes our way, as it may reveal issues that God wants us to address.

STOP

How do you think we, as Christians, should respond to stressful situations?

 'So I tell you this, and insist on it in the Lord, that you must no longer live as the Gentiles do, in the futility of their thinking' (Eph. 4:17).

 'For you were once darkness, but now you are light in the Lord. Live as children of light (for the fruit of the light consists in all goodness, righteousness and truth) and find out what pleases the Lord' (Eph. 5:8-10).

These verses tell us not to live the old way, but the new way— God's way. We are to live motivated by God's grace. Basically, what Jesus did should have an impact on us. It should motivate us. The way that we deal with stresses and struggles should be different now that God has saved us.

If we really belong to Jesus, we should be different.

STOP

So how can we learn how to deal with things better?

'Anyone who listens to the word but does not do what it says is like someone who looks at his face in a mirror and, after looking at himself, goes away and immediately forgets what he looks like' (James 1:23-24).

When we read the Bible and rely on God's Word, He helps us to see the truth about what's really going on in our lives. When everything goes wrong, the devil wants us to run as far and fast as we can away from God.

But as we've talked about, we can't hide anything from God. He wants our struggles out in the open. He calls us to own our sinful behaviour—not to get defensive, but to take responsibility. This is better than it sounds, honest!

God wants to drive us back to Him in repentance because God's forgiveness causes us to change and grow.

Our stresses and our sufferings are not unimportant; they have a purpose. *God uses them to produce perseverance and steadfastness in us.* They help us love each other better. When we've personally suffered loss and been hurt, we're more likely to be empathetic and compassionate.

There's one more thing: struggles reveal who's a real Christian and who's a fake Christian. When the going gets tough, the fake Christians pack their bags and walk away from God. In the Christian world, we would say God uses trials to separate the *'wheat from the chaff.'*

'Not everyone who says to Me, "Lord, Lord," shall enter the kingdom of heaven, but he who does the will of My Father in heaven. Many will say to Me in that day, "Lord, Lord, have we not prophesied in Your name, cast out demons in Your name, and done many wonders in Your name?" And then I will declare to them, "I never knew you;

depart from Me, you who practice lawlessness!'" (Matt. 7:21-23, NKJV).

When the stresses of life cause us to recognise that something is wrong, we need to run to Christ. We need to preach the gospel to ourselves, daily reminding ourselves of His grace. In doing so, He helps us to *'own it,'* to admit our sinful behaviour and not get defensive. God doesn't send trials to punish us or to prove He doesn't love us anymore. Instead, He sends trials for His good purposes.

 'And we know that in all things God works for the good of those who love him, who have been called according to his purpose' (Rom. 8:28).

KEY POINT
Suffering is a reality. We can't escape it. It's just a part of life.

MEMORY VERSE
'Blessed is the man who remains steadfast under trial, for when he has stood the test he will receive the crown of life, which God has promised to those who love him' (James 1:12, ESV).

SUMMARY
Trouble and trials happen. Some are just part of life, and others come because we've been planks and made some bad life-choices. The devil wants to use these times to separate us and keep us as far from God as possible, wallowing and continuing in our sin. This is a scary place to be—ultimately, we risk walking away from God. God, on the other hand, cares for us, and He uses trials to highlight things in us that need to be dealt with—things we need to repent of. He uses trials to grow and change us. To build in us perseverance so that we stand firm, not giving way no matter what life chucks at us.

WHAT'S THE POINT?

'Fear of Man' is where we fear people's opinions more than God's.

6. FEARING MAN MORE THAN GOD

Fear of man, in a nutshell, is when we replace the fear of the Lord in our life with fear of people. Sometimes, we call this 'peer pressure' or 'people-pleasing.' But whatever we call it, at the heart of it, *people matter more to us than God.*

What we fear tends to be what rules us. We might not think we have an issue with this—maybe we think we don't let anyone's opinion bother us. But it's likely not the case. Whether it's our mum or dad, our partner, our best pal, or even our neighbours, all too often we worry about what people will think. This might even lead us to change our behaviour and opinions.

There is a guy named Ed Welch who wrote a book called *When People Are Big and God Is Small*. In this book, he says, '*Fear of man is such a part of our human fabric that we should check for a pulse if someone denies it*'.[1]

 BIDDY

Biddy is standing in the queue at the checkout when she spots Mona. There's a moment when Biddy realises that if she just takes one step backwards, Mona won't even notice her. After hovering for what feels like forever, Biddy not only steps back but

---

1   Edward T. Welch, *When People are Big and God is Small: Overcoming Peer Pressure, Co-dependency, and the Fear of Man* (Phillipsburg, NJ: P&R Publishing, 2012), p. 17.

actually turns around and heads up the toilet roll aisle. When she stops, looking at the toilet rolls like they are the most interesting thing in her life, she mentally kicks herself. 'Why am I being such a numpty—Mona's my pal!' Biddy knows the answer to the question even before the thought has finished crossing her mind. She'd lied for Sean and she knew it wasn't right. She knew, because the guilt was eating her up inside. Every time she saw someone from church, or even passed the building, her stomach twisted. Mona wasn't daft. She had to know what people were saying, and Biddy just couldn't face her.

 'Fear of man will prove to be a snare, but whoever trusts in the LORD is kept safe' (Prov. 29:25).

STOP

Ask yourself these questions:

Have you ever struggled with peer pressure?
Do you care too much what people think about you?
Do you feel that you need respect from people?
Are you always second-guessing what you're doing because you're wondering what others think?
Are you afraid of looking bad?
Do you lie to people, especially those little white lies, to cover up something silly, to be funnier or even to make you look better?
Are you always comparing yourself to others?
Do you avoid people, especially when you think you've messed up?

The question we want to be thinking about is a simple one: Who's controlling us? If it's people and not God, then in some way we give people the right to tell us what to feel, think, and do. Now, I'm not saying we are being brainwashed into some kind of mindless zombie. What I'm saying is that their opinion and influence are so significant that we allow it to alter our behaviour.

> **STOP**
>
> *Whose opinion do you care about the most? Are there times when what they think affects what you're doing or thinking?*

 'Then Saul said to Samuel, "I have sinned. I violated the Lord's command and your instructions. I was afraid of the men and so I gave in to them"' (1 Sam. 15:24).

One translation actually puts it like this: *'I have indeed transgressed the command of the Lord and your words, because I feared the people and listened to their voice'* (NASB). Basically, he is saying, 'I've sinned against you, Lord, because I cared more about people's opinions than yours. I listened to what they wanted, and I did it.' They led him down the wrong path, and he ended up sinning against God. He wasn't actually fearing for his life or anything— it wasn't even peer pressure—he simply cared more about what they thought than God, and it had heavy consequences for him. So, it's important to think about whose voices you're listening to and what influence they have in your life. (See First Steps Book 3—*Voices*, if you haven't already read it.)[2]

 BIDDY

Biddy hasn't been a Christian for long, but she knows that lying to the police about Sean was bad. When Sean first told her to do it, she didn't think she had a choice. It's not like he forced her or anything. But you just don't grass on your kids to the police. It's not right! But she can't get wee Alice's face out of her mind. Every time she pictures the cuts and bruises, it makes her sick, thinking about the fact that Sean could do something like that. Still, that didn't stop the lie. At the end of the day, she protected her own, and that's the right thing to do. Right?

---

2   Andy Prime, *Voices: Who am I listening to?* (Fearn, Scotland: Christian Focus, 2019).

Willie pops in to see her one night. He knows straightaway something is up, and asks her about it. Biddy is reluctant at first, but eventually she has to tell someone. *'I don't really want to tell you—you're not going to like it. I was cleaning out my bag and found the Bible Mona gave me. It made me think about her. I miss her, but I've been avoiding her. Anyway, I flipped through the pages and stopped randomly at this bit—Leviticus 19. As I started to read, verse 11 slapped me in the face. "Do not steal." "Do not lie." "Do not deceive one another." I slammed it shut and shoved it back in the bottom of the bag. My insides have been in knots ever since. Willie, I lied to the police about Sean being here the night old Alice was done over. I've lied to everyone, even wee Alice, and she knows it. I think maybe I should have told the truth or said nothing. I can't take this anymore; it's eating me alive. And Sean, he makes me sick. I'm ashamed he's mine. I think I need to tell the truth for wee Alice's sake.'*

Willie just looks at her like he doesn't recognise her. *'Ma, are you being serious? Don't be stupid. No matter how much of a rat Sean is, you of all people can't grass on him to the police. You're his ma! I'll deal with him. He needs sorting out. He knows better than to bring you into his mess. You need to throw that Bible into the bin, where it belongs, and remember who your real family are!'*

STOP

What do you think of Willie's advice? Think of the last time you gave in to unhelpful voices in your life. Why did you listen to them more than God?

Biddy is clearly fearing people's opinions more than God's. She hid up the aisle from Mona, lied to the police, and is ignoring God. She knew it was wrong—even before she opened her Bible, she was feeling guilty and her conscience was pricking her. Despite that, she's struggling to do the right thing because she knows that if she does then she may be rejected by her family and the wider community.

Many of us do the same thing. We crave the approval of others. We fear their rejection, their condemnation, and their anger. We feel that we need them to accept us, And, just like Biddy, we're controlled by these desires.

Often, it's a particular individual or type of person whose approval we crave: parents, friends, a spouse, the pastor, or a person in power like our boss. We wouldn't admit it directly, but our behaviour and language reveal the way we need and want *something* from them—their love, respect, approval, praise, or acceptance.

I've talked a lot in this book about idols—things that are more important to us than God. When it comes to fear of man, surprisingly, *the underlying idol is actually us*. I know you might have expected me to say other people, but **when we crave approval, love, acceptance, assurance, and affirmation, we're basically asking them, in a twisted way, to worship us.** It's all about us!

Are we beginning to recognise the influence of fear of man in our lives? Now we need to think through how we deal with it.

> **STOP**
>
> *How do you think you would deal with Biddy's dilemma?*

We need to go to God, seek forgiveness and ask for His help. Not only does He forgive the truly repentant, but He will help us to resist the temptation to keep on doing it.

We need to remember who it's all about—God—and learn to think on Him.

'For you have been called to live in freedom, my brothers and sisters. But don't use your freedom to satisfy your sinful nature. Instead, use your freedom to serve one another in love' (Gal. 5:13, NLT).

This is something that I have struggled with off and on for years. It doesn't have the hold on me it once had years ago, but I'm not foolish enough to say that I have conquered it completely because I know that's asking for trouble. Over the years I've recognised my weaknesses more quickly and I've learnt to run to God before they've become an issue. Basically, I try to be mindful, engage my brain and make sure I have good accountability. If we don't get a handle on this, it will continue to get more deeply embedded in our hearts and habits, and unless we run to Christ in repentance and prayer, people will always matter more to us than God.

STOP

I leave you with the question: 'What has been more important to you than God this week?' What is your honest answer?

We cannot allow fear of man to rule us. We need to run to God, repent, rely on Him and ask Him to help us deal with this crippling idol.

KEY POINT

When we replace the fear of the Lord in our life with the fear of people instead, what we fear tends to be what rules us. Instead of our lives being ruled by God, we are ruled by people and their opinions.

 ## MEMORY VERSE

'Fear of man will prove to be a snare, but whoever trusts in the LORD is kept safe' (Prov. 29:25).

SUMMARY

When we replace the fear of the Lord in our life with fear of people, it's an issue. Whoever it is—whether it's our mum or dad, our partner, or our best pal—all too often we worry about what people will think. This might even lead us to alter or change our behaviour and opinions to suit them and not God. We don't want to end up like Saul, saying 'I've sinned against you, Lord, because I cared more about people's opinions than yours. I listened to what they wanted, and I did it. They led me down the wrong path and into bother with God.'

WHAT'S THE POINT?

We need to learn how to deal with conflict in a godly way.

7. DEALING WITH CONFLICT

BIDDY

Biddy is standing at the bus stop, waiting on the number 30 bus. Just before the bus is due, a couple start to approach the bus stop. It's clear they aren't happy. As they draw nearer, she can actually hear the heated discussion that is going on. They are having a fight about who is looking after their kid that day. Biddy feels sad for the little girl walking beside them and thinks to herself, '*This poor thing is going to feel like she's not wanted if they don't shut up.*' Even as they get on the bus, they get louder and louder. At one point, she thinks the driver is going to get up and chuck them off the bus.

'*A gentle answer turns away wrath, but a harsh word stirs up anger*' (Prov. 15:1).

When we hear about conflict, our minds automatically jump to the big stuff, like the screaming match Biddy observed on the bus or a punch-up in the street. But not all conflict involves throwing punches; in fact, much of the conflict that exists between us is much more subtle. Let's think that through for a moment as we reflect on our Facebook post that went wrong,

or the text we sent that was misinterpreted,

or the harsh email we sent without thinking it through,

or the backhanded comment,

or the banter that went too far, or the sarcastic remark that was meant to get our point across,

or that pointed joke laced with just a little too much truth.

The sad thing is that when it comes to conflict, it's not just confined to the world; Christians can be guilty of it, too. It might not be as obvious or violent as throwing punches or smashing someone over the head with a baseball bat. But snide comments, harsh words, raised voices and backbiting are but a few examples of subtle conflict you may see among Christians, especially online!

Conflict is inevitable, which means we need to think it through. We need to understand conflict, what's really going on and how to deal with it well. We need to understand it from a biblical perspective, and learn how to handle it in a godly way.

STOP

Think about a recent conflict—one that wasn't violent or shouty. What kind of long-term impact do you think it caused?

STOP

Why do you think conflicts arise?

In the world, when it comes to conflict, it's all about the resolution: coming up with a solution in which two opposing desires can live in harmony with each other. But is that actually possible? Can two people with legitimate yet irreconcilable desires both get what they want?

I doubt it.

But to get past the clash, someone—or, more realistically, both parties—will have to compromise in some way, shape or form. It's a matter of give and take as they negotiate some kind of peace or truce.

The reality is that this peace treaty may be tentative. Even if a compromise has been reached, all it takes is one little shift in desire, a hint that the other person isn't toeing the line or stepping up to the mark, and the conflict fires back up again. The truce is not a permanent solution, but a precarious plastering over the situation.

We can easily see how this becomes a big business. After all, further conflict-resolution meetings are required, and further compromises and reassurances are dished out for the cycle to begin again. No wonder UK businesses spend over £33 billion a year on it.[1] It's a self-perpetuating business that never gets to the root of the problem. Why? Because the world diagnoses the problem wrongly and so ultimately it never resolves conflict for the long term.

Basically, the world offers a skin-deep solution for a deep-rooted problem.

 'Because human anger does not produce the righteousness that God desires' (James. 1:20).

> **STOP**
>
> *What do you think the real problem is? Why are people constantly in conflict?*

To really think this through, we need to look at what the Bible has to say, and when it comes to conflict there seems one clear place to go, the book of James. Look at verses 4:1-2. James is pretty clear about what's at the heart of conflict.

---

1   <https://www.cedr.com/news/?item=Conflict-is-costing-business-GBP-33-billion-every-year>. Date accessed 28th August 2019.

'*What causes fights and quarrels among you? Don't they come from your desires that battle within you? You desire but do not have, so you kill. You covet but you cannot get what you want, so you quarrel and fight. You do not have because you do not ask God*' (James 4:1-2).

James is very clear about what causes us to quarrel and fight: *we don't get what we want*. We fight because our desires—what we want—are being scuppered by someone or something.

In that moment, our lusts and cravings are ruling our lives.

They're in competition with someone else's, which is why conflict erupts. Ultimately, when this happens, our desires directly compete with God's rule in our lives.

I want to think this through a little. It's not as though desire by itself causes conflict; instead, it's the status we give to our desires that causes conflict. The desire itself might be an innocent one, even a good desire, but we twist it. When our idols are threatened and when we don't get what we want, conflicts, quarrels and fights come. The world may view our desires as legitimate, but that's not how the Bible sees their rule in our lives.

It's like we are saying, '*My will be done, and woe betide you if you get in my way.*'

 BIDDY

The last few weeks, Biddy has been back at church and reading her Bible. But most important of all, she has sorted it out with God and said sorry. She knows what she has to do; she just doesn't really want to do it. She has been dreading the conversation with Sean, but it has to be done. Sitting at the table, playing with her dinner, she eventually starts, '*Sean, I have been thinking about this for a while and I know you're not going to like what I have to say, but I can't lie for you about Alice. It's not right and God doesn't want me to.*'

Sean rages. As he slings his dinner across the table, the plate smashes into pieces. He screams at his mum, *'WHAT! I'll tell you what I think about your GOD!'* Grabbing his mum, he screams and shouts right in her face, threatening her with all sorts. Biddy is sobbing uncontrollably, but even she never expected what happened next. The back of Sean's hand came right across her face so hard she felt her teeth rattle. The sheer force of the blow sends her flying. The next second seemed to last minutes as they just stared at each other, both stunned at what he'd done. Then he just walked out the door. Biddy knew then that she couldn't have him back in the house.

STOP

Think of the last time you had a moment with someone where you quarrelled or fought. How did you respond?

 'A gentle answer turns away wrath, but a harsh word stirs up anger' (Prov. 15:1).

Think through the conflict and ask yourself one of my favourite questions: *'What did I want that I didn't get?'* or *'How am I playing God and asserting my own will?'* Ultimately, we have to ask ourselves the even harder question: *'How am I loving and obeying God in this—and am I loving my neighbour at all?'* That one might sting a bit.

When it comes to conflict, it may be true that the other person was being a complete idiot. They may have even said the worst thing we have ever heard and behaved like an uncaring fool. But that doesn't excuse our behaviour. We can't tell God that *they* made us say it, think it or do it.

God helps us understand our part in any conflict. What we brought to the table reveals how our twisted desires are really at the heart. James reminds us that when our motivations are wrong, we become enemies of God:

'When you ask, you do not receive, because you ask with wrong motives, that you may spend what you get on your pleasures. You adulterous people, don't you know that friendship with the world means enmity against God? Therefore, anyone who chooses to be a friend of the world becomes an enemy of God. Or do you think Scripture says without reason that he jealously longs for the spirit he has caused to dwell in us?' (James 4:3-5).

But it's not all doom and gloom.

'But he gives us more grace. That is why Scripture says: "God opposes the proud but shows favour to the humble"' (James 4:6).

This is amazing. Do you see the promise? God gives us more grace. **His grace is greater than our sin.** When we go to God in repentance, He amazingly gives us His grace, forgiveness and mercy. James doesn't actually explain how that grace comes; he assumes we know that Jesus humbled Himself to the cross, died and rose again. James reminds us that in Christ, He helps us to handle any situation—even conflict.

'Submit yourselves, then, to God. Resist the devil, and he will flee from you. Come near to God and he will come near to you. Wash your hands, you sinners, and purify your hearts, you double-minded' (James 4:7-8).

> **STOP**
>
> *So, how should we deal with conflict better?*

In James 4:1-8, he gives a couple of practical pointers which help us deal with conflict well.

Firstly, *press pause and recognise what's really going on.* Are we being a me-centric person who's twisting and distorting the truth to our own advantage?

Basically, is the problem *us?*

In the middle of any conflict, we must be searching out what's going on with our sinful heart. I'm not saying we can never be righteously angry, but that would be the exception rather than the rule. In the main, when conflict takes place, there are two sinful hearts fighting for something they each want.

 'When you ask, you do not receive, because you ask with wrong motives, that you may spend what you get on your pleasures' (James 4:3).

Secondly, James clearly reminds us that *we should pray.* That doesn't mean we just pray for what we want and then get cheesed off that we didn't get it. No, we should pray about what's really going on. Recognising our sin and our need for God drives us back to Him in repentance and prayer. He gives us the strength to resist the temptation and obey His will.

 'If your brother or sister sins, go and point out their fault, just between the two of you. If they listen to you, you have won them over. But if they will not listen, take one or two others along, so that "every matter may be established by the testimony of two or three witnesses". If they still refuse to listen, tell it to the church; and if they refuse to listen even to the church, treat them as you would a pagan or a tax collector' (Matt. 18:15-17).

Lastly, Matthew 18 is clear how we deal with conflict. But let's be clear: Matthew doesn't say:

> *If your brother or sister sins against you, go ahead and complain about them behind their backs. Yes, you're right to stop talking to them. Yes, you're right to absolutely grow angry toward them,*

HOW DO I MAKE THINGS RIGHT? ◆ 81

gossip about them or plan to get them back—after all, eye for an eye and all that.

No! Matthew doesn't suggest any of these things. He's very clear—if we have an issue with a brother or sister, prayerfully go see them one-to-one. If that doesn't work, take a mature believer with you and speak to them again. At this point, if there's still an issue and nothing is working, then speak to the elders, who will pray and advise and finally take it to the church if necessary.

But all of this must start with a one-on-one conversation.

Many of us might not know if we've offended others. After all, mind-reading isn't a spiritual gift. So in these moments, we must show others the grace and mercy God has shown us. We must think well of them and deal quickly with any matter. Don't give the devil an inch because if you do, he will turn that tiny pimple of a harsh word into a mountain of regret.

STOP

How do you think God can use our moments of conflict for gospel witness?

KEY POINT

We have all been involved in some kind of conflict. We need to learn how to deal with it in a godly and helpful way.

MEMORY VERSE

'The words of the reckless pierce like swords, but the tongue of the wise brings healing' (Prov. 12:18).

SUMMARY

We've all had moments of conflict, times when we would instantly undo the hurtful words we've said the moment they're out our mouth. All too often, we don't engage our brains, and so we end up hurting people. Whether intentionally or because of blind stupidity—conflict happens. Usually, we want something we aren't getting. We need to learn to deal with conflict by showing others the grace, patience and kindness that Christ shows us.

WHAT'S THE POINT?
Sometimes God asks us to try and fix what we have broken.

8. PUTTING IT RIGHT

'Sorry' may be the hardest word to say. It's a word we not only have to say to God, but also to people we have hurt. When our relationships are shattered, we need to try and put them right—this might even mean relationships from before we were Christians.

This is probably one of the most significant chapters in this book. In the last chapter we looked specifically at how to deal with conflict, and touched briefly on some biblical principles we find in Matthew. Read the passage again for review:

'If your brother or sister sins, go and point out their fault, just between the two of you. If they listen to you, you have won them over. But if they will not listen, take one or two others along, so that "every matter may be established by the testimony of two or three witnesses". If they still refuse to listen, tell it to the church; and if they refuse to listen even to the church, treat them as you would a pagan or a tax collector' (Matt. 18:15-17).

In this chapter, we're going to look at restoration. Now, if you're anything like me, when you hear the word 'restoration' you think of one of those TV programmes where a couple take on a derelict building and, through blood, sweat and a lot of tears, restore it to its original state at great personal expense. It's usually a three-year nightmare of stressful battles for them, but sixty minutes of light entertainment for us.

'Restoration' means the act of returning something to its original condition or repairing it so that it functions well, but maybe in a new way.

As Christians, when we talk about restoration, we aren't talking about some crazy building project, but our personal relationships that need to be restored and made right.

'Repent, then, and turn to God, so that your sins may be wiped out, that times of refreshing may come from the Lord, and that he may send the Messiah, who has been appointed for you—even Jesus. Heaven must receive him until the time comes for God to restore everything, as he promised long ago through his holy prophets' (Acts 3:19-21).

Before we were Christians, our relationship with God was totally fractured, and we were separated from Him because of our sin. But Jesus, through His death on the cross, brought reconciliation between us and God. A guy called Paul Tripp said, 'The greatest work of human relationships is not the pursuit of human happiness but reconciliation to God.'[1] Therefore, we are no longer separated from God, but are made children of God, brought into His family, having been totally forgiven. *Yes, yes, I know this, I heard you say it the first time.* So why am I telling you again? Because we forget—and we need to remember.

'Restore to me the joy of your salvation and uphold me with a willing spirit' (Ps. 51:12, ESV).

Even though Christians are completely forgiven for past sins, God may ask us to try and restore something that has been broken. Let

---

1   Paul Tripp, 'Speaking Receptively' (*The Journal of Biblical Counselling*, 16:3, Spring 1998).

me drive that home a bit more directly. Before we were Christians, we probably did some horrendous things to people. Some of our relationships may be completely shattered, perhaps forever.

'Sorry' might be the hardest word to say, but it might not be enough to restore the trust of someone we've significantly hurt for years. It might take time for them to see that you have truly changed. You might have to accept they may never trust you again—it can't be fixed.

> ### STOP
>
> *Do you think saying sorry is enough to heal all of the wounds you have inflicted?*

Before you make a huge list of names and start knocking on lots of doors, speak first to a wise, mature Christian or one of your elders about this. Share who you think you need to speak to, why the relationship is broken, and ask them for wisdom and prayer. If you were the abuser or a consistent offender, then approaching someone—even with the right intentions to beg for forgiveness— would probably terrify them. You may actually make things worse in your attempt to start making things better.

I suppose what I'm trying to say is, *be wise.*

 BIDDY

Biddy and Mona are sitting at the kitchen table for their weekly one-to-one. They have been meeting for ages now, and they talk about almost everything. Mona has tried to talk to Biddy about Sean and never gets very far. Today, she tries again. *'Biddy, there's something I want to talk to you about, and I know you're going to find it hard to hear—I want to talk to you about Sean.'*

Biddy hasn't forgiven Sean. Even thinking about that night, she instinctively wants to touch her face. Sean hit her so hard she'd had a massive bruise and swollen cheek for days. When her other sons found out, it was all she could do to stop them from beating him senseless. She made them promise, and they only agreed as long as she didn't let him back in the house. To be honest, she didn't really need persuading. She realised he couldn't come home after that. She was scared of her own son. *'Mona, I don't want to talk about this.'*

'Sweetie, please listen to what I have to say. I know it's hard, but it's important, or I wouldn't bring it up. You know Sean has been coming to the evening service, but he's also been meeting up with Andy for Bible study for months and coming to all the morning prayer meetings. Last night, he became a Christian, and Andy thinks he's genuine.'

There was silence for a long time before Biddy spoke. 'Well, you've told me. Now I don't want to talk about it anymore!'

The relationship between Biddy and Sean has been totally shattered by Sean's violent behaviour and most definitely needs to be restored. It's important for so many reasons, but if Biddy refuses to forgive and make peace with Sean, she will be hurting her relationship with God.

 'Therefore, I tell you, her many sins have been forgiven—as her great love has shown. But whoever has been forgiven little loves little' (Luke 7:47).

STOP

If you were in Biddy's shoes, could you forgive Sean? Do you think there are any relationships God might want you to try and restore?

BIDDY

Sean is sitting with Andy having a brew. They've been talking about his mum for about the hundredth time. *'Andy, I don't know how long I can keep avoiding her. I think I have to move away; it would just be the easiest thing for both of us. She's never going to accept I might have changed.'*

STOP

What do you think Sean should do? How do you think he should speak to his mum?

'Be completely humble and gentle; be patient, bearing with one another in love. Make every effort to keep the unity of the Spirit through the bond of peace' (Eph. 4:2-3).

It would be so much easier if we could just walk away, like Sean wants to do, but that wouldn't be the best thing for him or his mum in the long run. It can be exactly the same way with us. It may be easier to just walk away and let sleeping dogs lie. Restoring any broken relationship is going to be hard. We must choose to love the Lord enough to want to do the difficult things He asks of us, not just because it's best for us, but maybe because it's good for them also.

'He restores my soul. He leads me in paths of righteousness for his name's sake' (Ps. 23:3, ESV).

STOP

What kind of advice do you think Andy should give Sean to help him speak to Biddy?

Thinking about how Sean should try and restore his relationship with Biddy should lead us to think about how we could begin to restore some of our own broken relationships. Here are some pointers.

- **Pray.** We must pray and ask God for wisdom and help before beginning the restoration process. Remember, what seems impossible to us is possible for God.

- **Make the first move.** No matter how much we might dread the thought of it, we are going to have to take the plunge when it comes to restoration. It will take courage for us to contact a person out of the blue. But the onus is on us to make the first move.

- **Rely on God.** He has given us constant access to Himself through prayer. He's given us His Word as a guide, the Holy Spirit to lead us in truth and other believers to help us along the way. Lean into and rely on God. He is trustworthy.

- **Say sorry.** It's actually surprising how disarming a real-life, genuine, heart-felt apology is. For many of us, especially if we've never apologized for a thing in our lives, it might get stuck in our throats. But it has to be done. We need to apologise without blame-shifting or accusation. Too often we are too prideful and stubborn.

- **Listen.** Really listen and hear what people have to say. Don't butt-in every five seconds to defend yourself. People need to feel listened to.

- **Be a peacemaker.** Respond, but do so with gentleness and love. We are bound to see things differently than them, so we have to be careful. Sometimes we just need to let things go. Remember, we're trying to bring about reconciliation, not reopen all wounds and start an argument all over again.

+ **Remember the purpose.** Reconciliation and healing broken relationships bring honour to God. Our ultimate objective is to model the Lord Jesus to those we have hurt in the past.

Relationships are hard work! Restoration can do so much more than give relationships a new start. One of the big things to think about is how this could witness to our non-Christian family and friends. Let's face it: before Jesus saved us, we were probably a real pain in the neck, causing havoc and trouble, thinking only of ourselves and often leaving a trail of hurt people behind us. Before coming to Jesus, it might have been completely out of character for us to say sorry and actually mean it.

This speaks of how much Jesus has changed us, and even gives us opportunities to share the gospel.

STOP

What do you think being a peacemaker really looks like? What parts of peacemaking are difficult for you?

 'Finally, brothers, rejoice. Aim for restoration, comfort one another, agree with one another, live in peace; and the God of love and peace will be with you.' (2 Cor. 13:11, ESV).

 ### BIDDY

Sean has been thinking about his mum for ages, and he and Andy pray about it nearly every morning. He knows he has to go and sort it out. There's no choice; he has to pluck up the courage and just do it. But if he's being really honest, he's terrified. Terrified she will just slam the door in his face. He remembers the moment he hit her, and he loathes himself. Surely, she hates him, too. Every day for a week now he's walked to his mum's door and turned back at the last second. He's here again, heart thudding in his chest, and he taps on the door. When it opens and he sees her face turn instantly from joy to fear, it devastates him. He's caused that. Then the words come out. *'Mum, I am so sorry…'*

STOP

Is it possible to forgive someone and to withhold reconciliation?

STOP

What if Biddy never restores her relationship to Sean? What kind of damage will that do to her, him and their family? What would it communicate about the gospel?

This is one of those *'what if'* moments. What do we do if we want to reconcile with someone, but they refuse point-blank? What does Sean do if Biddy shuts the door? It's not like we can pin someone down and force them to forgive us. As my wee mum would say, *'You can take a horse to water, but you can't make it drink.'*

So what can we do? We can be faithful to God and try our best. If they refuse, then we must accept that graciously. We can pray for them regularly and pray that the Lord softens their heart and gives us another opportunity. But we can't force them into doing what we want.

We must pray, wait and trust God.

KEY POINT

As Christians, restoration should follow any conflict we have with each other. However, even though God has completely forgiven us for our past, there are times when He also asks us to restore relationships we've harmed—both before we became Christians and afterwards.

MEMORY VERSE

'*Brothers, if anyone is caught in any transgression, you who are spiritual should restore him in a spirit of gentleness. Keep watch on yourself, lest you too be tempted*' (Gal. 6:1, ESV).

SUMMARY

Even though we are completely forgiven for our past sins, God may ask us to try and restore something that has been broken. 'Sorry' may be the hardest word to say, but it might not be enough to restore the trust of someone that we've significantly hurt for years. It might take time for them to see that you have truly changed. You might have to accept they may never trust you again. Nonetheless, we pray, wait and trust God.

WHAT'S THE POINT?
We need to make sure we honour God in all relationships: single, dating or married.

9. SINGLENESS, DATING AND MARRIAGE

I know it seems strange to have this as the last chapter, especially as most would expect it to be the place we'd start. The truth is, I wanted to think through the big picture of relationships before I touched on the specifics.

Having a relationship can throw up a lot of questions for the new believer. Can Christians date anybody they like? Can they 'try before they buy'? What does dating look like for Christians? What are the *rules* and how do they work?

What about marriage? What does a good Christian marriage look like? There's so much we could say about this. So brace yourself; it's going to be a bit of a whistle-stop tour.

 ILLUSTRATION

I remember listening to a guy who said that when he dated for the first time as a Christian, he didn't know how he was supposed to act at the end of the night. Should he shake her hand or kiss her? He opted for patting her on the head! I know, really?! She obviously found it endearing because they are married now!

STOP:

What do you think are some of the pressures facing single people today—inside and outside the church?

If you're new to the Christian life, then being single from a biblical perspective can be a bit weird. It's totally different from the way the world does things, and probably nothing like you are used to. One of the big changes to think through is that sexual activity of any kind is only for marriage. So no more drunken one-night stands, no 'friends with benefits.' Things are different for Christians. God asks us to save ourselves for marriage, to be pure.

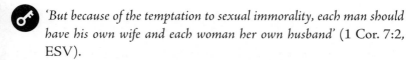 *'But because of the temptation to sexual immorality, each man should have his own wife and each woman her own husband'* (1 Cor. 7:2, ESV).

Of course, our temptations don't just go away overnight.

We live in a hugely sexualised culture. Sex sells, and we see it everywhere: TV shows, films and advertising. If we're already struggling with sexual temptation, watching a movie which is overtly sexual and detailed can cause us to be tempted and lead to sins such as masturbation, watching porn or casual sex.

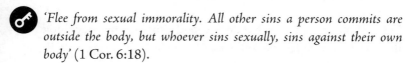 *'Flee from sexual immorality. All other sins a person commits are outside the body, but whoever sins sexually, sins against their own body'* (1 Cor. 6:18).

STOP

Do you think there is anything you watch that could be unhelpful?

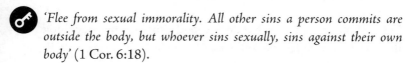 *'For this reason a man will leave his father and mother and be united to his wife, and the two will become one flesh. So, they are no longer two, but one flesh'* (Mark 10:7-8).

When we have sex with someone, we become united with them.

The Bible calls it 'one flesh.' In other words, sex is never casual. The Bible is clear that sex is an act of intimacy and self-commitment that involves the *whole* person. Sexual immorality affects our relationship with Jesus, ourselves and others—including our future spouse. Sex is powerful, and if we sleep around then we do untold damage to ourselves.

Are you starting to grasp how important this is? When I became a Christian, I had been seeing my then boyfriend since I was fifteen years old. I didn't sleep around, but I wasn't a virgin either. When we both became Christians, we stopped. I'm not saying we weren't tempted—I'd be lying to you if I did—but we had to obey Christ. It didn't matter that no one else would know because, ultimately, we knew God would have known. We just couldn't carry on, no matter how much we wanted to.

 'It is God's will that you should be sanctified: that you should avoid sexual immorality; that each of you should learn to control your own body in a way that is holy and honourable, not in passionate lust like the pagans, who do not know God' (1 Thess. 4:3-5).

> **STOP**
>
> *Have you been struggling with this? Is God challenging you about flirting with sexual sin?*

Before we start to think about dating, I want to pause just for a moment and think about how we do friendship with the opposite sex.

> **STOP**
>
> *Do you think that men and women can be friends?*

Friendship without thought is one of my pet hates. I'm not saying we have to avoid the opposite sex, but we need to engage our brains. If we aren't careful, we can actually hurt people we care about by our thoughtlessness.

If you're flirting with a guy or girl because it makes you feel good and strokes your ego, then stop being a plank before they get hurt.

If you're being all exclusive, having wee private chats just the two of you, then stop being a plank before they get hurt. I've seen too many people get hurt because of a thoughtless friendship.

 ILLUSTRATION

I remember a girl who was seriously flirting with guy friends she had, regardless of how they felt and even when she knew they were attracted to her. She was being reckless with their feelings, and it was a mess of pain waiting to happen. When I challenged her, she denied any flirting or wrong doing. I remember saying to her, 'Would you speak to Andy or Mez like that?' (Two married pastors in our church.) She was affronted and instantly said 'No, I would not!'

Engage your brain and don't be a thoughtless friend. Can men and women really be friends? I don't think this is really a straightforward 'yes' or 'no' answer. Yes, they can be friends with wisdom and solid boundaries in place. When we aren't wise, it can make for a confused and painful mess.

What about dating? I know this sounds a little bit mental, but the Bible never actually mentions the word dating—or 'courting,' as my wee mum used to call it. People were either single, engaged, or married in the Bible. There didn't seem to be a period of time where they dated before being engaged or anything like that.

Does that mean dating is ruled out? I don't think so. The Bible doesn't say that dating is a sin, but it does give us helpful principles.

I know this might seem controversial in this day and age, but until you're mature enough to marry, I'd suggest you shouldn't be dating. Neither do I think Christians should date for dating's sake. If you're not ready to marry, then don't date until you are.

STOP

Why do you think I would say that?

The thing is, there might be issues that need sorting. You may be watching porn; you may be struggling with same-sex attraction; maybe you consider yourself bi-sexual; maybe you've been with three partners before and have a couple of kids; perhaps you have never been in a faithful relationship; maybe your ex cheated on you. There may be sin, pain and baggage you need to deal with before you think about sharing in someone else's sin, pain and baggage.

 ## ILLUSTRATION

Sean really struggles with porn and has for a long time. He started with a few images, but before long he had a subscription to an adult channel and watched every night—and it was getting nastier. Masturbation was a given when he watched; he used it as a tool to relieve stress. After he became a Christian, the struggle continued, but he has had some moments of victory. He took a bit of time to be honest about all this with his one-to-one, Andy, but eventually he came clean with the whole miserable truth.

Sean has a bit of a soft spot for Rebecca. She is a lovely girl, and he has been thinking about asking her out.

STOP

Do you think Sean is ready to think about asking Rebecca out? How would you speak into his life?

Obviously, Sean has a bit of growing up to do before he would be in a place where he is mature enough to consider dating—never mind marrying—anyone.

So what should we be looking for in a potential date? I'm not saying you shouldn't fancy them, but it shouldn't be what rules us. Hear me out. They might be the cutest person on the planet, but if they don't have solid Christian character and a real love for the Lord, then run a mile.

When considering someone to date, think about their character, integrity and faithfulness to the Lord.

How do they deal with trials?

Are they servant-hearted?

What do their prayers reveal about their faith?

I'm not saying that you should interrogate them, but you do need to think about more than the colour of their eyes and how tall they are. I'd also suggest that it's helpful to ask some advice from a mature Christian who knows you—and listen to what they say.

> **STOP**
>
> *We all have a secret list in our head about what our spouse should look like. What does that look like for you, and how central is biblical character?*

So, they have the three G's (God, Grace and Good Looks) and you start dating and it gets serious. The chaste kiss at the end of an evening turns into passionate snogs. The question has to be tackled:

How far is too far? Where's the line?

I can tell you now that if you ask ten different Christians you'll get ten different answers. Oh, don't get me wrong, everyone will agree on no sex before marriage, but there is a massive spectrum in between. No one would have an issue with holding hands, but there would be debate on passionate kissing and heavy petting. There are Christians out there that would even suggest oral sex is okay before marriage as it's not exactly penetration sex (of course, they are deluded, and are justifying their sinfulness with lies, so don't even think about it!).

I read a really interesting book by a guy called Kevin DeYoung called *The Hole in Our Holiness*[1] and he talks about this. Basically, he says that unless we're married, we shouldn't do anything with a girl/boyfriend that we can't do with any other Christian. At first, I thought that was a bit extreme. So not even one kiss then? But he basically says that we need to care for them as a brother or sister and protect each other from temptation. The more I think about this, the more I agree with this type of intentional, loving care.

When dating, we need to think about more than just *who*, but also *how* we date in a God-honouring way.

As we move into the next part of this chapter, dating becomes marriage.

For some Christians, this might be hard to hear. But the Bible is very clear that Christians must only marry Christians, which also means that Christians must only *date* Christians. And, I mean a real Christian, not just someone who is happy to be dragged to church.

 'Do not intermarry with them. Do not give your daughters to their sons or take their daughters for your sons' (Deut. 7:3).

> **STOP**
>
> *Do you think that's harsh? What problems can you see occurring in a relationship between a Christian and an unbeliever?*

---

1   Kevin De Young, *The Hole in Our Holiness* (Wheaton, Il: Crossway Books, 2014).

A non-Christian won't understand why Jesus is so important to us. We'll want to live as a Christian by dealing with our sin, and an unbeliever won't even admit that they have sin to deal with. We won't be on the same page with anything: kids, tithing, service... I've known people who have married non-Christians and, within a short space of time, they don't even go to church anymore. We can tell ourselves all sorts of lies like, '*If I date them, then they'll be drawn to God and become a Christian.*' But 'flirt to convert' very rarely works!

'*Do not be yoked together with unbelievers. For what do righteousness and wickedness have in common? Or what fellowship can light have with darkness? What harmony is there between Christ and Belial? Or what does a believer have in common with an unbeliever?*' (2 Cor. 6:14-15).

 ILLUSTRATION

Mona has a good friend, Caroline, who has been a really active Christian and involved in church. Then she met Tom at work. He's as nice as they come, but wasn't interested in God in any way. When Caroline started dating Tom, Mona took her for coffee, shared her concern and spoke about what the Bible said. Caroline struggled with what Mona said and thought the verses she used were not for today. Caroline struggled even more when her minister refused to marry them at church, advising her against it altogether.

Caroline knew her church family loved her. She just couldn't understand why they wouldn't accept Tom. She decided the best thing to do was to change churches. She did, and she got her big wedding.

She still sees many of her old friends from church and meets up with Mona every month. She is happily married now and has two little kids. She and Tom have had some struggles in their marriage. They just seem to come from different ends of the spectrum. Some of her biggest struggles have been in the way she brings up her children. Caroline wants the kids to know about God from a very young age, but Tom thinks it's pointless. He really feels that she and the kids should be staying home on Sundays because it's 'family time.'

> **STOP**
>
> *How would you have had that conversation with Caroline? Do you think Mona was just meddling in Caroline's business?*

Marriage seems to have lost the significance it once had. Some people feel marriage is outdated—it's just a piece of paper. Some people get married because they are lusting after sex; some because they are lonely; some because they are desperate for kids; and so forth. We need to make sure we're getting married for the right reasons. All too often, people marry unwisely and are 'unhappy-ever-after.' After all, marriage isn't for our convenience or until we get bored. It's a lifelong relationship.

 'The LORD God said, "It is not good for the man to be alone. I will make a helper suitable for him"' (Gen. 2:18).

When we think about Genesis 2:18, we see that it's not good for man to be alone, and God's solution was to provide him a wife in Eve. Marriage was created to be a loving relationship between one man and one woman. It was created as the only place for sex. It was created as the best place for raising children. But it was also created so that husband and wife might have a deep friendship based on love and trust. Marriage is about so much more than sex. It's about companionship.

> **STOP**
>
> *(Single readers) Has marriage become an idol for you? How are you using your singleness as a blessing for you and your church family?*

> **STOP**
>
> *(Married readers) Do you see your spouse as your best friend? Is marriage what you expected? How do you fail to measure up to your own ideal?*

Like all marriages, Christian marriages face trouble. That's why it's so important that they are firmly grounded in the Bible. Too many Christians have this romantic idea of marriage, but it's hard work. In any marriage there are two sinful, selfish people coming together, and that's going to cause issues that need dealing with. Marriage needs to be driven by the Lord, and that means making Him a priority in our lives. It's about how we sacrificially love our spouse, putting them first instead of our own desires.

A pastor named Alistair Begg puts it like this: *'The greatest joy we will experience in marriage is found when we learn to put our partner first. When we value the happiness of our spouse over our own happiness, we will begin to understand the meaning of true, sacrificial love.'*[2]

 'Dear friends, let us love one another, for love comes from God. Everyone who loves has been born of God and knows God. Whoever does not love does not know God, because God is love' (1 John 4:7-8).

There's so much in marriage I could focus on, but we haven't the space for that. Simply put, I want us to see that marriage, at its heart, shows a picture of who God is. Marriage is about God and His love for us; it's about how we love each other because of that. The more we start to understand God's love, the more we realise that, apart from Him, we are basically incapable of truly loving anyone the way we should.

---

2   Alistair Begg on Ephesians 5:22-23. 'Planting Hedges in Marriage, Part Two', November 17, 1996. <https://www.truthforlife.org/resources/sermon/plntng-hedges-in-marr-pt-2/>. Date accessed 28th August 2019.

'We love because He first loved us' (1 John 4:19).

Because He loves us, we are to imitate His love *'and live a life of love, just as Christ loved us and gave himself up for us'* (Eph. 5:1-2).

Tall order, right?

It's so much more than just wanting to live happily ever after. If we're not ready to do that, or if we're not mature enough to want to kill our selfish desires, then I'd ask if we are really ready for marriage. If you aren't sure, ask the advice of mature married people in your church. Chat with your accountability partner before seriously thinking about pursuing marriage.

Ask, pray and *listen*!

KEY POINT

Single, dating or married: we need to put God first, trust in Him and be content in whatever situation He has placed us. In every relationship, we need to learn how to sacrificially love others. As we learn to love God more, I pray we learn to love ourselves less, and in doing so love those around us better.

 ### MEMORY VERSE

'But godliness with contentment is great gain. For we brought nothing into the world, and we can take nothing out of it' (1 Tim. 6:6-7).

 ### SUMMARY

I've been thinking about how to end this book, and there seems only one way to do it: with a prayer. Let's all pray that we love God more, ourselves less and others better.

IX 9Marks

This series of short workbooks, from the 9Marks series, are designed to help you think through some of life's big questions.

GOD: Is He Out There?

978-1-5271-0296-5

WAR: Why Did Life Just Get Harder?

978-1-5271-0297-2

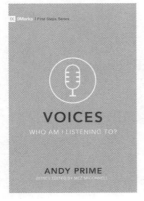

VOICES: Who Am I Listening To?

978-1-5271-0298-9

BIBLE: Can We Trust It?

978-1-5271-0000-8

BELIEVE: What Should I Know?

978-1-5271-0305-4

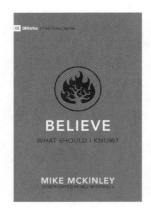

CHARACTER: How Do I Change?

978-1-5271-0101-2

TRAINING: How Do I
   Grow As A Christian?

978-1-5271-0102-9

CHURCH: Do I Have To
   Go?

978-1-5271-0426-6

SERVICE: How Do I Give
   Back?

978-1-5271-0472-3

IX 9Marks

Building Healthy Churches

9Marks exists to equip church leaders with a biblical vision and practical resources for displaying God's glory to the nations through healthy churches.

To that end, we want to see churches characterized by these nine marks of health:

1   Expositional Preaching
2   Biblical Theology
3   A Biblical Understanding of the Gospel
4   A Biblical Understanding of Conversion
5   A Biblical Understanding of Evangelism
6   Biblical Church Membership
7   Biblical Church Discipline
8   Biblical Discipleship
9   Biblical Church Leadership

Find more titles at

www.9Marks.org

2⊕schemes
Gospel Churches for Scotland's Poorest

20schemes exists to bring gospel hope to Scotland's poorest communities through the revitalisation and planting of healthy, gospel-preaching churches, ultimately led by a future generation of indigenous church leaders.

> *'If we are really going to see a turnaround in the lives of residents in our poorest communities, then we have to embrace a radical and long-term strategy which will bring gospel-hope to untold thousands.'*
>
> **MEZ McCONNELL,** Ministry Director

We believe that building healthy churches in Scotland's poorest communities will bring true, sustainable, and long-term renewal to countless lives.

THE NEED IS URGENT

Learn more about our work and how to partner with us at:

20SCHEMES.COM
TWITTER.COM/20SCHEMES
FACEBOOK.COM/20SCHEMES
INSTAGRAM.COM/20SCHEMES

Christian Focus Publications

Our mission statement —

STAYING FAITHFUL

In dependence upon God we seek to impact the world through literature faithful to His infallible Word, the Bible. Our aim is to ensure that the Lord Jesus Christ is presented as the only hope to obtain forgiveness of sin, live a useful life and look forward to heaven with Him.

Our books are published in four imprints:

CHRISTIAN
FOCUS

Popular works including biographies, commentaries, basic doctrine and Christian living.

CHRISTIAN
HERITAGE

Books representing some of the best material from the rich heritage of the church.

MENTOR

Books written at a level suitable for Bible College and seminary students, pastors, and other serious readers. The imprint includes commentaries, doctrinal studies, examination of current issues and church history.

CF4•K

Children's books for quality Bible teaching and for all age groups: Sunday school curriculum, puzzle and activity books; personal and family devotional titles, biographies and inspirational stories — because you are never too young to know Jesus!

Christian Focus Publications Ltd,
Geanies House, Fearn, Ross-shire,
IV20 1TW, Scotland, United Kingdom.
www.christianfocus.com